GIFTS FROM THE MODERN PANTRY

GIFTS FROM THE MODERN PANTRY

Healthy Homemade Treats for Any Occasion

RACHEL DE THAMPLE

PHOTOGRAPHY BY ALI ALLEN

BETTERWAY BOOKS

CONTENTS

INTRODUCTION

WHY MAKE EDIBLE GIFTS?

Food, more than any other gift, is one you can engage with on so many levels. It doesn't just look pretty (although, I hope you'll agree that all of the recipes in this book are as beautiful as they are tasty), it stirs all your senses. The fragrance of jasmine truffles or the sweet spices from a jar of mango chutney. The texture of melt-in-the-mouth olive oil shortbread, the delicious chewiness of cardamom banana chips, or the crunch of a cauliflower beer pickle—one of my favorites!

Edible gifts also provide a thoughtfulness you just can't get from something shop bought. I love connecting presents with moments I've shared with the recipient. Indeed, many of these recipes were crafted as a consumable capsule of a specific memory. The roasted chestnut biscuits were inspired by a picnic in a local park just beyond the park's avenue of ancient chestnut trees. Foraged, roasted and baked into biscuits, I froze them to give at Christmas. The rose honey came from the most fragrant and velvety red rose I'd ever seen from my friend's allotment and honey from a local beekeeper. The coffee-infused vinegar was inspired by lovely early summer afternoon with my friend Sara foraging for elderflowers. I've also been inspired by gorgeous friends who've made me beautiful edible gifts, which I've been desperate to recreate myself.

Pouring love and thought into a present and taking a moment away from your busy life to really think about who is receiving it is so much more enriching than stressing around the shops looking for a shoe that probably won't quite fit.

WHAT IS THE MODERN PANTRY?

The idea of a modern pantry is of course completely open to interpretation, but for me and those I spoke to about it, the words "healthier," "faster," "small batch," "less waste," "resourceful" but also "gourmet," "creative" and "fun" arose. I've kept these things in mind here. I also have a bit of a reputation for being thrifty, but in a way that is modern and gourmet at the same time. Those who've tried my banana skin vinegar, strawberry top shrub or preserved lemons will attest! Seasonality is also key. My adventures in the kitchen are inspired by nature's larder, and even better are gifts made from things you've grown, gathered or sourced locally.

To me, food should be as nourishing as it is delicious. Taste is always my priority, but I think homemade will always be healthier than something that's shopbought or processed. Certainly, some recipes are healthier than others, but if you can provide a delicious gift that has added benefits or a treat people can consume without any conflict, then it makes the offering so much richer.

PACKAGING IDEAS

Edible gifts are the ultimate statement of creative consumption on so many levels, one of which involves packaging. I've been completely guilty of making beautiful biscuits, chutneys or jams for friends and then dashing off to a shop to buy something pretty to wrap them in. I wouldn't go as far as to say this defeats the purpose. By no means does it, but there are lots of ingenious ways to make the most of what you've got to package your homemade gifts, and doing so will add more of a personal touch.

Here are just a few ideas:

- Use old magazine pages or scrap paper as wrapping or to make origami boxes. For magazines you can use pages with photography of beautiful produce, interesting recipes or articles relating to the gift or the interests of the receiver. If using paper, you could always adorn it with a poem, a quote or a simple drawing.

- The silver, gold or bronze paper from chocolate wrappers is brilliant for repackaging chocolates or biscuits, or for crafting gift tags.

- Fabric is also brilliant to wrap gifts in or cap jars. You can either reuse scraps of old material, buy feet of new fabric (or cheesecloth, which is brilliant if your friends will use it in the kitchen, too) or use beautiful tea towels, which make lovely packaging.

- Always reuse ribbons, and it's also lovely to reuse old wrapping paper. On a few occasions, I've received a present housed in some lovely paper I'd sourced and used—I loved the fact that my friend thought it was beautiful enough to save for another use—and I loved getting it back so I could then employ it for another gift.

- Pottery, old vintage tins or pretty jars—ones you've either sourced or reused—are perfect for edible gifting.

- Mixing bowls are also fun to bundle biscuits in, as are pretty plates wrapped with a lovely napkin or tea towel for an added layer of gifting.

PERFECT GIFTS FOR ALL OCCASIONS

BIRTHDAYS: Homemade Worcestershire sauce, Oak-aged chili sauce, Coffee balsamic

GET BETTER: Nourishing pot noodles, Rose honey, Kombu-chai, Classic sauerkraut

CHRISTMAS: Christmas kraut, Honey-fermented cranberries, Sloe gin & Slider, Roasted chestnut snowballs

EASTER: Honey bunnies

NEW BABY: Persian pistachio butter cups

NEW HOUSE: Nourishing pot noodles, Homemade Worcestershire sauce, oven-dried tomatoes

LEAVING PRESENT: Craft malt vinegar

ROMANCE: Rose honey, Persian pistachio butter cups, Quince honey butter

HOUSEGUEST: Roasted raspberry jam, Homemade tahini, Veryan's molasses granola, Blood orange & rhubarb marmalade

DINNER INVITE: Sanchia's pickled ginger, Jasmine truffles, Victorian apple jam

PICNIC: Herb garden lemonades, Peach & lavender butter, Sicilian shortbread, Rustic jam tarts

FOODIE FRIEND: Hoisin plums, Smoked beetroot pickles, Cowgirl kimchi, Banana skin vinegar, Horseradish salt, Persian dried limes & beldi lemons

GARDEN PARTY: Rosé kefir

BEREAVEMENT: Mayan chocolate biscuits, Lavender & lemon verbena tea, Marmalade & toast truffles, Chocolate hazelnut spread

SUMMER BBQ: Polish dill pickles, Cauliflower beer pickles, Strawberry top shrub

KID-FRIENDLY: Cream soda kefir, Chocolate hazelnut spread, Apple cinnamon digestives, Peanut butter & banana biscuits, Roasted plum leathers, Cardamom & lime banana chips

COCKTAIL PARTY: Garden gins, Horseradish vodka, Turkish coffee kombucha, Persian Lemon pistachios

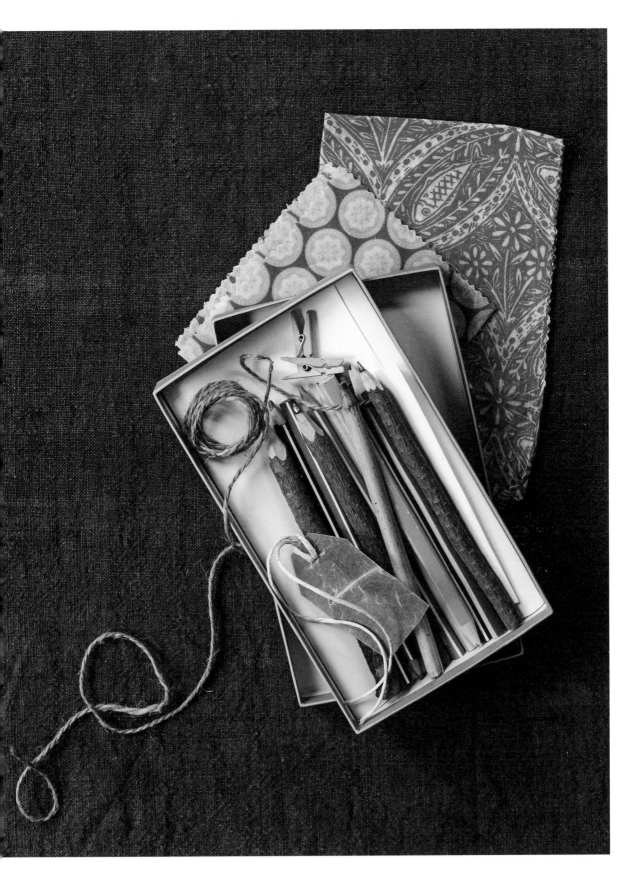

INFUSE

Infusing is one of the easiest ways to preserve food. All you need to do is bundle the fruits, flowers or herbs you want to capture into a sterilized jar (see page 78) with a preserving medium like vinegar, sugar, salt, honey or booze. Vinegar is by far the healthiest, and the result of adding fruits, herbs and spices to it is stunning.

Submerge your flavors of choice fully and let them mingle in your chosen medium—be in vinegar, sugar, salt, honey, booze or other drinks like homemade lemonade—until you get the depth of flavor you're after. The more fruit, flowers or herbs you add, the faster you'll get your desired results. Taste often and strain as soon as the flavor is right for you. Then sweeten a little, if you like, to soften and round out the flavors.

COFFEE BALSAMIC

I'd recommend using decent-quality vinegar for this—supermarket own-label organic balsamic vinegar is often a good choice. It doesn't need to be the aged or thick and syrupy type. I've gone for a small portion as this is a great way to use up spent coffee grounds left over from making your morning coffee. I hate waste, so this is a gorgeous way of putting the usually discarded grounds to good use. You could also use fresh coffee grounds for the richest flavor and the fastest infusion.

Makes 250ml

6 tablespoons coffee grounds (used or fresh)
250ml balsamic vinegar

Spoon the coffee grounds into a clean jar. Cover with the vinegar and secure with a lid. Shake every day or so to help the flavors mingle together.

Strain the mixture using a cheesecloth-lined sieve after a week, or longer if you want a richer coffee flavor—you can infuse for up to a year. Decant into a nice bottle.

Give this to your favorite coffee-loving friend with a list of suggested uses—it's delicious with roasted beetroot, as a marinade for steak or as a salad dressing, added to a homemade barbecue sauce, or mixed in equal quantities with butter and maple syrup or brown sugar and coat a fresh batch of popcorn.

CHERRY PIP VINEGAR

Cherry pips have a wonderful almondy flavor and this is such a delicious way of embracing them and ensuring they don't go to waste. Once matured, this vinegar makes a brilliant base for salad dressings, or you can add a drop to a smoothie (or any dish) in place of lemon juice for a little acidic kick. Plum and apricot stones also make brilliant infused vinegars that turn waste into a gourmet gift. Make sure you only use whole, uncracked pips.

Makes 200ml

3–4 tablespoons cherry pips, or
  enough to half fill a 250ml jar
200ml apple cider vinegar or white
  wine vinegar
1–2 tablespoons sugar, maple syrup
  or clear honey

Pop the cherry pips straight into a sterilized jar (see page 78) and cover with the vinegar.

Steep for at least 6 weeks or up to 1 year—the longer the steep, the stronger the almondy, cherry flavor will be.

Strain, sweeten to taste, and decant into a clean bottle or jar. It will keep indefinitely.

If you have a fruit-loving friend, make individual batches using cherry, plum and apricot stones, and give them a trio of flavors to experiment with.

WILD VINEGARS

I'm mad about foraging. What attracts me most is how seeking wild food really connects you with nature. You start to look around more and notice nature's little nuances as each season unfolds. I especially love foraging in an urban environment where you could easily get lost in concrete and commercialism and instead you end up being seduced by the quirkiness of plants that can grow anywhere and produce beautiful food in the harshest environments. These delicacies are worth treasuring, and there are two really easy ways to do so: infusing your finds in vinegar or alcohol.

Effectively, you're producing a flavored vinegar (or booze) and you can use pretty much any fruit, herb, flower or spice, but the ones below are by far my favorites—and ones I shed a tear over when I part with my last drop. Choose one flavor, or experiment and mix your own!

Makes 1 bottle

choice of flavoring (see below)
white wine vinegar, cider vinegar or
    rice vinegar
sugar, clear honey or maple syrup,
    to sweeten

FLAVOR OPTIONS

elderflowers and elderberries
horseradish roots, roughly chopped
    or fresh horseradish leaves
fig leaves or ripe figs, quartered
ripe blackberries
wild garlic leaves or wild garlic
    seeds

*Decant the vinegar into a lovely
vintage bottle and add a paper
tag for a personal touch.*

Fill a clean jar or bottle at least one-third full of fruit, roots, leaves or flowers and fill to the top with your choice of vinegar—white wine, cider or rice. For darker, richer fruits like blackberry and elderberry, you can use a richer vinegar like red wine, balsamic or sherry vinegar.

If you want the flavors to infuse into the vinegar faster, add more of your chosen flavor to the bottle, filling it half full or a little more.

Leave to infuse for at least 1 month, then taste and see how it's getting on. Leave for longer if you want a stronger taste. Once infused to your liking, strain the steeping ingredients out—if you've used fruit, like blackberries or figs, you can use them as pickles in salads or on a cheeseboard instead of just discarding them.

Decant the strained, flavor-infused vinegar into a clean bottle and, if you like, sweeten it with a little sugar, honey or maple syrup to soften the harshness of the vinegar. You could also use alternative sweeteners such as stevia or xylitol, which are ideal for diabetics. The vinegar will keep for years, but is best and most fresh if consumed within 1 year.

WORCESTERSHIRE SAUCE

There are few savory dishes that a dash of Worcestershire sauce can't transform. I love it in stews, soups, on cheesy toast, splashed over steak, a few drops added to a Bloody Mary or even just dotted over fresh or roasted tomatoes. It's a wonderful store cupboard staple, and offering up a homemade version as a gift makes it an even more cherished ingredient. Make sure you whip up enough sauce so you can have a stash of your own.

Makes 3500ml

125ml malt vinegar
125ml apple cider vinegar
150g blackstrap molasses
2 tablespoons tamarind paste
1 tablespoon soy sauce
1 teaspoon ground black pepper
1 cinnamon stick
6 whole cloves
¼ teaspoon cayenne pepper
4 shallots or 1 medium onion, finely
   chopped
4 garlic cloves, finely chopped
2 teaspoons freshly ground ginger
8 anchovies or sun-dried tomatoes
   (for vegan option), finely chopped
juice of 1 lime

Place all the ingredients in a sterilized lidded jar. Stir to fully mix together.

Set in a cool, dark place to infuse for 1–2 weeks (or longer for a stronger flavor). Taste and adjust the spices, seasoning to suit your taste with more pepper, salt, vinegar or sweetness.

Strain through a cheesecloth or fine-mesh sieve. Decant into sterilized bottles. Keep at room temperature for up to 3 months if you've used anchovies, or up to a year if you used sun-dried tomatoes.

ROSE HONEY

A cheats rendition of rose water, this is a stunning way of capturing the fragrance of summer roses. The redder the roses, the pinker your honey will be—but you can use any color blooms. It makes a fantastic ice cream too—whisk 4 egg yolks with 4 tablespoons warmed rose honey until the yolks have thickened, whisk in 300g double cream and freeze until firm. It's utterly delicious.

Makes 200g

200g clear honey
large handful of fresh, fragrant
  unsprayed rose petals

Place the honey in a saucepan. Gently heat, just until warmed through. Gently stir the rose petals through, crushing them a little to help release their natural oils and flavor. Cover and allow to steep for at least 1 hour, or overnight if possible. Strain through a fine mesh sieve or cheesecloth, squeezing out as much honey as possible. Spoon into a sterilized jar. It will keep for years.

LEMON OIL

The trick with making infused oil (be it chili, lemon, orange or a herb oil), is to use dried produce. Fresh chilies, zest or herbs can dilute the preserving qualities of the oil and could lead to the growth of botulism, which is not something to mess with. Dried oil infusions, however, are safe and often impart a richer flavor. This oil is a brilliant ingredient for dressing salads or finishing dishes.

Makes 250ml

2 lemons
250ml olive oil (use a good-quality
  but mildly-flavored oil)

VARIATIONS

Use strips of dried zest from
2 oranges or 2–6 dried chilies,
to taste, in place of the lemon

Strip the zest using a vegetable peeler and try to just get the zest and not the white pith. Dry at room temperature for 3 days or in an oven at 100°C/212°F for 45 minutes until fully dried.

Add the zest to the oil. Infuse for 2–6 weeks, then strain and decant into a clean bottle. Best used within 1 year.

HERB GARDEN LEMONADES

I helped set up a community garden in my local park and I spend a lot of time there in the summer, picking herbs and flowers like lemon verbena, lavender, Moroccan mint, pineapple sage and more. We used to have a lot of picnics in the garden and when we did, we would bundle some of these fragrant flavors into bottles of homemade lemonade. They make the most amazing gifts for summer parties and picnics.

Makes 1 liter

4 lemons
3–4 tablespoons clear honey or
   maple syrup (or golden caster
   sugar)
fresh herbs or edible flowers
   (see below)

HERB AND FLOWER OPTIONS

5 sprigs lemon verbena
5 sprigs Moroccan or garden mint
12 pineapple sage leaves
3 sprigs rosemary (with the blossom
   if in season)
7 sprigs lemon balm
4 elderflower heads
handful of fresh, fragrant rose petals
   or 3 tablespoons dried rosebuds
4 sprigs fresh lavender (leaves and
   stems)

Use a vegetable peeler to take a few strips of peel from one of the lemons. Halve and juice all the lemons, including the one you used for the peel. Strain out any lemon seeds. Whisk in the honey, adding more or less to taste—3–4 tablespoons is the perfect amount in my view.

Taste and pour into bottles, then add the zest and herbs or flowers. Give it all a good shake and refrigerate for 1–2 hours, or overnight, to infuse the flavors. I leave the herbs and flowers in the bottle as they look so pretty, but strain before serving if you prefer.

If you want an instant infusion, you can blend the herbs with the lemonade and strain them out, sweeten and bottle.

TIP: *Use any unused zest from the lemons to make Lemon Oil (page 22).*

Make a few bottles of different flavors and take along to a summer BBQ or garden party for the host.

STRAWBERRY TOP SHRUB

This shrub was inspired by an article I read about making the most of strawberry tops—the green stem and leaves you normally lop off and toss out. Infused in vinegar along with the tough woody stems from mint, the combination produces a flavor not far off that of the classic English summer fruit punch mix called Pimm's—albeit, a very healthy version.

To drink, simply strain the fruit out (you can eat it—try it in salads) and pour into a tumbler with ice. Top up with sparkling or good-quality tonic water. You can also add a shrub shot to a smoothie or use it to make virgin cocktails.

Makes as little or as much as you'd like

handful of strawberry tops
a few mint sprigs
enough apple cider vinegar
  to cover
a little sugar or clear honey,
  to sweeten

Pile the strawberry tops into a sterilized jar (see page 78). Add the mint sprigs. Pour in enough vinegar to fully cover—press the mint down into the jar, if needed, to ensure it's submerged.

Secure the lid and leave to mature in a cool, dark place for 2–3 weeks or up to 1 month. Strain the strawberry and mint out and sweeten to taste. This will keep at room temperature for more than 1 year, but I like to store mine in the fridge so it's cold and ready to drink.

HORSERADISH VODKA

River Cottage is an amazing organic smallholding in Devon, England, where I teach preserving and fermentation courses, and I think my horseradish vodka won over the chefs there. I brought a bottle along to my first ever class and the head chef got so excited about it, so I gave him a bottle, which he used in a beef consommé. It's amazing in a Bloody Mary or even as a shot on its own. For a non-alcoholic version, infuse horseradish root (or leaves) in apple cider vinegar or white wine vinegar, giving you a brilliant base for salad dressings, mayonnaise (lovely with smoked mackerel fishcakes) and more.

Makes 750ml

8cm piece of fresh horseradish root
750ml vodka
2 strips of fresh or dried lemon zest
  (optional)
2 juniper berries (optional)

Peel the horseradish and cut into 4–5 pieces. Pop it into a bottle with the vodka. Add the lemon zest and juniper (if using).

Infuse for 4–6 weeks before straining and decanting into clean bottles. It will keep for years but is best consumed within 1 year.

This is a great gift for a Bloody Mary lover. Create a little cocktail kit packaging this Horseradish Vodka with a bottle of nice tomato juice, celery salt, homemade Worcestershire Sauce (page 20) and Oak-aged Chili Sauce (page 40). Talk about the ultimate Bloody Mary!

GARDEN GINS

I love making seasonal and garden-inspired gin infusions, and have gained a bit of a reputation for them. I often get asked to create new flavors as welcome drinks for various events. My favorite gin infusion at the moment is lemon verbena, but I also adore fig leaf and rose petal gins. Below are my top seven favorite garden-inspired gins, but do go "off-piste" and create your own as well.

This recipe makes 750ml, but you can easily scale it down by dividing one bottle of gin to make smaller portions each with different flavors.

Makes 750ml

750ml gin (ideally an organic gin
  with basic botanicals)
choice of garden flavors
  (see below)
a little clear honey, sugar or
  alternative sweetener, to taste
  (optional)

FLAVOR OPTIONS

12 sprigs fresh lemon verbena
2–8 fig leaves
2 handfuls fresh black currant
  leaves (new spring leaves are the
  best)
2 handfuls fragrant rose petals
2 handfuls ripe rosehips
5 stalks fresh rhubarb, chopped
5 large elderflower heads

Simply bundle your gin and garden flavors into a clean jar or bottle. Leave to infuse at room temperature for 4–6 weeks. Shake the contents once or twice a week to help release the flavors.

Strain and decant into clean bottles and sweeten to taste, if you like. Consume within 1 year.

Give a bottle to a gin lover along with a side of their favorite tonic.

SLOE GIN & SLIDER

This is a wonderful two-for-one recipe as the strained sloes can be made into a second drink called Slider, and both make great Christmas gifts. Traditional sloe gin recipes call for equal amounts of sugar to sloes, but I've used less sugar, which gives a deliciously dry finish. If you prefer syrupy, port-like sloe gin, double up on the sugar.

Sometimes you need to add equal quantities of sugar to fruit and that is because some fruits (such as fresh juicy oranges or lemons, or summer berries and stone fruits like raspberries and peaches) will dilute the preserving qualities of the alcohol, and if you don't add enough sugar to turn those juices into a shelf life-friendly syrup, the drink will start to ferment and could spoil. Sloes are quite dry, as is rhubarb, which means you can easily get away with using less sugar.

Makes 750ml

300g ripe sloes
150g sugar
750ml gin

FOR THE SLIDER

300g gin-infused sloes
500ml apple cider

Prick each fruit a few times with a fork or the tip of a small knife. Alternatively, freeze the sloes. This makes the fruit swell and burst, which means you don't have to puncture the skins by hand.

Once pierced or frozen, mix the sloes with the sugar. Set aside for 1 hour to help draw out some of the juices, creating a bit of a sloe syrup.

Cover with the gin and store either in one large jar or bottle, or divided into smaller bottles, ensuring the sugar and sloes are equally distributed. Shake every week or so and leave to infuse for 6–8 weeks (or up to 1–2 years, for a really mature flavor). Strain and decant into clean bottles, but keep the strained sloes to make Slider (see below).

SLIDER

Place the infused sloes into a clean jar or bottle and cover with the cider. Leave to infuse for 4–6 weeks.

Strain and decant into clean bottles. This is best consumed within 2 weeks after it's fully infused. You can offer it as a gift with the sloes still in it. It's delicious on its own as an aperitif.

FERMENT

Fermentation is a brilliant, super-healthy way to preserve food. Consuming fermented food daily is a great way to keep your gut healthy. Fermented foods also add boundless flavor to meals and are as fun to make as they are to consume.

A really easy method is lacto-fermentation. The word lacto refers to lactic acid. All fruits and vegetables have beneficial bacteria, such as lactobacillus, on the surface. Providing the right conditions (typically by adding salt and packing in an air-tight container) these bacteria convert sugars into lactic acid, which inhibits the growth of harmful bacteria, increases the amount of good bacteria and acts as a brilliant preservative. It also gives fermented foods their characteristic sour flavor. Lacto-fermented pickles are delicious, simple and don't require a lot of special equipment or ingredients—plus they have the benefit of homemade probiotics.

Another way to kick start fermentation is to add a culture such as a kombucha SCOBY, an apple cider vinegar mother of kefir grains to what you'd like to ferment. All of these starters house a variety of beneficial yeasts and bacteria. Scoby stands for Symbiotic Culture of Bacteria and Yeast, and it will look like a disc of jelly. You can find it online at www.happykombucha.co.uk. Shop-bought bottles of raw apple cider vinegar will come with the mother which will look like little cloudy strands in the liquid, and kefir grains can be bought online and stored at home to use multiple times.

CLASSIC SAUERKRAUT

When it comes to fermenting veg, this is the place to start, with a humble cabbage and a big spoonful of salt. It really couldn't be easier, and the transformation that happens in just a few days is something to behold. Serve kraut swirled through a batch of simply cooked Puy lentils with garden herbs, and leftover shreds of meat from a Sunday roast. A perfect offering for friends or family who are housebound in the winter months, but need the boost of fresh veg to keep them healthy.

Makes about 500g

1 cabbage (white, green or red), 2 outer leaves reserved and the remainder thinly shredded, core discarded

2 apples, skin on, coarsely grated sea salt

1 tablespoon caraway, cumin or fennel seeds, or freshly grated ginger or horseradish (optional)

Weigh the shredded cabbage and apples. Add 2 percent of the weight in salt, so for every 100g cabbage add 2g salt. Combine in a big bowl and add the spices (if using). Massage and scrunch the cabbage and apple until it releases a bit of liquid.

Transfer the cabbage into a sterilized jar (see page 78) little by little, packing down each layer as you go so the brine rises above the veg. The key is to ensure you keep as much air out as possible.

Use the reserved cabbage leaves to cover the compacted cabbage. Press down until there's a good layer of liquid covering it (the brine will kick-start the fermentation). You want enough brine to come right up to the top of your jar. If the cabbage hasn't released enough liquid of it's own, mix up a quick brine to top it up by whisking 50ml water with 2g sea salt. Pour this over the top until it comes right to the top of the jar.

Secure with an airtight lid and keep in a dry place at room temperature. Leave to ferment for 5–7 days until the tang and tenderness are to your liking. The longer you leave the cabbage the more vinegary and tender it will be. You can leave it for 2 weeks or more if you like.

Once you're happy with the flavor, move to the fridge to stop it fermenting further. As long as it's fully covered in the brining liquid it will keep for months in the fridge.

CHRISTMAS KRAUT

Get ahead with your Christmas dinner with this delicious, good-for-your-gut sauerkraut with a festive twist. It beats braised cabbage hands down and is brilliant with leftovers on Boxing Day and beyond.

Makes 500g

1 red cabbage, 3 outer leaves
   reserved and the remainder
   finely shredded, core discarded
2 eating apples, cored and finely
   diced
sea salt
1 tablespoon freshly grated ginger
½ teaspoon mixed spice
¼ teaspoon ground cinnamon
pinch of ground cloves (optional)
grating of nutmeg (optional)
juice and zest of 1 clementine
2 bay leaves
1 cinnamon stick
2 star anise

Pile the cabbage and apple into a large bowl with the salt, ginger and spices. Scrunch together for 5 minutes, or until the mix releases about 6 tablespoons of juice. Mix in the clementine zest and juice. Weigh the mixture and calculate 2 percent sea salt—so for every 100g mixture add 2g sea salt.

Pack the kraut into a 750g–1 liter sterilized jar (see page 78) tucking the bay leaves, cinnamon stick and star anise in around the edges of the jar. Tightly pack the cabbage, adding it little by little and pressing it down to help release more juices. Cover with the reserved leaves, pressing down so you get all the juices on top and no floaty bits of cabbage—remove any bits that escape or tuck them back into the mix. If the cabbage didn't produce enough bring to come right to the top of the jar, mix 50ml water with 2g sea salt and pour over the cabbage leaf-capped kraut until the brine comes right up to the top of the jar.

Secure with an airtight lid and leave at room temperature in a warm, dark place for 5–7 days, or as long as 2 weeks. Check every so often to ensure the liquid still covers the mixture.

Once you're happy with the flavor, pop it into the fridge until ready to eat.

For an extra-special gift, give someone a batch of spicy, zesty kraut along with a stoneware fermentation jar.

COWGIRL KIMCHI

I've called this cowgirl kimchi as I've added some smoky notes by using chipotle-smoked chilies in place of fresh ones as well as smoked paprika, a wonderfully accessible alternative to the traditional Korean red chili powder, or *gochugaru*, which gives kimchi its authentic reddish appearance. Packed with A, B and C vitamins, kimchi will make the perfect companion to campfire cuisine and a perfect gift for cowgirls who enjoy the smoky outdoors.

Makes about 650g

1 large white cabbage, 3 large
  outer leaves reserved and
  the remainder quartered, core
  discarded
1 liter filtered or mineral water
40g sea salt
1 chipotle chili or about
  1 tablespoon chipotle chili flakes,
  depending on how hot you want it
4 garlic cloves, peeled
2 tablespoons freshly grated
  peeled ginger
1 tablespoon smoked paprika
1 pear, finely diced or coarsely
  grated

Cut the cabbage wedges into 2cm thick slices. Whisk the water and salt together in a large glass or ceramic bowl. Submerge the cabbage in the liquid, cover with a clean tea towel and set aside for 8–12 hours or overnight—during this time the veg will take in beneficial yeasts and bacteria from the air.

Grind the chili, garlic and ginger to a paste in a small spice grinder or a pestle and mortar. Alternatively, finely chop everything together. Mix in the smoked paprika.

Drain the cabbage and reserve the liquid. Mix the chili paste and pear through the cabbage, then pack the mixture into a sterilized jar (see page 78), pressing it down as tightly as you can, ensuring there are no air pockets. Cap the mixture with the reserved cabbage leaves, tucking the leaves in at the sides so they form a lid of sorts to hold everything down. Pour over enough of the reserved brine to come right to the top of the jar. Seal with an airtight lid and set on a plate to catch any juices that might bubble out as it ferments.

Leave to ferment in a dark place for 7–10 days, checking it daily to ensure it stays fully submerged in the liquid. Try not to open the jar, though. After a week, give it a taste. When it's tender and tangy enough for your liking, it's ready to eat. You can ferment it for up to 3 weeks, and the longer you leave it, the more sour it will be.

Enjoy straight away or store in the fridge in a sealed, sterilized jar until you're ready to eat it. As long as it's covered in brine and stored in a clean jar with an airtight lid, it will keep for months if not years.

OAK-AGED CHILI SAUCE

My granddad always had an assortment of homemade chili sauces on the table with every meal, which is probably where I get my love for chili. He never made this fermented version, but it's something I've come to absolutely love—and it's so outrageously easy to make. You just need a little patience. The woodchip addition is completely optional, but it lends an extra layer of flavor and is a cheat's way of getting a barrel-fermented flavor. A chili lover's gift, if ever there was one!

Makes 150–200ml

100g red chilies, thinly sliced, seeds and membranes removed if preferred
2 garlic cloves, thinly sliced
2 tablespoons oak or apple wood chips (optional)
300ml filtered water
1 tablespoon sea salt
clear honey or maple syrup, to sweeten (optional)

Spoon the chili and garlic into a small lidded jam jar (about 340g).

If using, toast the wood chips in a dry frying pan over a high heat for about 1 minute until they release a smoky aroma. Spoon into a 12cm square of cheesecloth and tie securely. Add to the jar, pressing down into the chili and garlic.

Whisk the water and salt together until the salt has fully dissolved. Add to the jar, filling it to the top, and secure with an airtight lid. Leave to ferment for at least 1 week, or until it starts to bubble a little and the chilies become tender. Ferment for 3–4 weeks for a tangier flavor.

Once fermented, remove the wood chip parcel and drain, reserving the liquid. Place the drained chili and garlic mixture in a food processor or coffee grinder with 3–4 tablespoons of the reserved liquid and blend until smooth, adding more of the brine as needed. Make it as thick or thin as you like—I like mine a little more textured than Tabasco. Strain out the solids, if you like, or leave them in. Sweeten with honey or maple syrup too, if you like.

Once it's to your taste, pour into a sterilized bottle (see page 78). Secure with a lid and store in the fridge for up to 3 months.

TIP: *If you've strained the mixture, dry the chilies and garlic on a baking tray at 100°C/212°F for 45-60 minutes. Once cool, mix with salt and use for rubbing into meat, veg or fish, mixing through butter or scrambled eggs. It can even be used in summery Mexican-style cocktails.*

HONEY-FERMENTED CRANBERRIES

For the past 10 or so years, I've been stocking up on organic cranberries grown on the island of Terschelling, which is part of the Netherlands. The season is late November, so I typically buy loads to preserve in preparation for Christmas and this has been my go-to recipe. It makes a beautiful gift. The quantities below are for one jar only, but it's easy to scale up, depending on how many fresh cranberries you can source.

Makes 340g

100g fresh cranberries, pricked all over with a fork or the tip of a knife
3 slices of fresh ginger, peeled
4 cloves or a pinch of dried rose petals or rose buds
2 tablespoons freshly squeezed orange or clementine juice
about 150g clear raw honey (or enough to fully cover the fruit)

Fill a sterilized jar (see page 78) with the cranberries, ginger and cloves, leaving about 2–3cm of space. Pour over the orange or clementine juice.

Pour in enough honey to fully cover the cranberries. It may take a while for the honey to make its way down to the bottom of the jar, so add some, wait for it to settle, then add some more. Cover the jar tightly and give it a few turns to coat all the berries in the honey.

Loosen the lid and put the jar in a dark place. Set it on a plate in case there is any honey overflow as it ferments, which is likely. Every few days tighten the lid and give the jar a few turns, then re-loosen the lid and return to the plate. Soon you will start to see bubbles forming.

The honey will turn a lovely red color and become thinner as time goes on. The cranberries will start to lose some of their tartness and will become a little wrinkled. These can be left to ferment for quite a while, several months even, and will be tastier as time goes on. The flavor, even after just a few weeks, is amazing too though.

You can eat the cranberries as they are, or blend them in a food processor into more of a jammy sauce. Delicious on toast, served alongside cheese, with meats, in salads or grain-based dishes with fresh herbs.

Pack these into a ceramic jar and wrap in a lovely cloth to add a personal touch to your gift.

CRAFT MALT VINEGAR

This is a really versatile gift—you can tailor it to different tastes depending on the beer. A malty beer will make malt vinegar, but you can also use a hoppy one or even stout. I love a craft red ale, but that's just me. It's great with fish and chips, in soups, stews, salads and as a marinade. Choose a friend's favorite beer and make the vinegar in the original bottle for a personal touch.

Makes 330–500ml

330–500ml bottle of craft beer
strands from an apple cider vinegar
  mother (optional, see page 32)

Open the beer and add the apple cider vinegar mother (if using). Cover with a breathable but tightly woven cloth and secure with string or a rubber band. Allow to ferment for at least 1 month if using an apple cider vinegar mother, or 2 months if not. You can ferment it for longer, just taste it occasionally to make sure it's not too sour.

Once you're happy with it, remove the cloth and secure with a lid.

BANANA SKIN VINEGAR

A brilliant way of using old banana skins and a delicious ingredient in ceviche, salad dressings, cocktails or smoothies. It has a wonderful sour, bitter flavor with an underlying sweetness.

1 banana will make about 150ml

fresh banana skins, finely chopped
150ml filtered or mineral water
20g golden caster sugar

Half fill a sterilized jar (see page 78) with banana skins. Whisk the water and sugar together until dissolved and pour into the jar. Cover with a cloth and set on a plate in a dark place for 2–3 weeks, stirring daily.

Once the liquid has become carbonated and less sweet, strain the liquid into a clean bottle. Cover with a clean piece of cloth and let it ferment for a further 2–3 weeks. Decant into a sterilized bottle. Secure with a lid and offer up as a gift, or keep for yourself!

SALT-PRESERVED CITRUS

This is one of the easiest and most delicious ways to preserve citrus fruits. The traditional variety used in Morocco is citron beldi, which are small and highly aromatic. Bergamot lemons, larger but with a similar fragrance, are also favored and blood oranges, Seville and navel oranges are all spectacular too. However, when I teach, it's always the limes that send people's tastebuds into an excited frenzy. Every. Single. Time. They start to think of all the possible uses: a slice in place of an olive in a "dirty" martini, rubbed into a shoulder of lamb with fresh coriander, used in a salsa verde as an alternative to anchovies. A jar of these aromatic beauties will be sure to delight, every time.

Makes 2 x 450g jars

1kg small, unwaxed citrus (limes, lemons, blood oranges, kumquats, Seville oranges, navel oranges, clementines, etc.)
150g good-quality sea salt
1–2 teaspoons chosen spice (such as fennel seeds, coriander seeds, star anise, crushed cardamom pods, cinnamon bark, cloves etc.)

Wash the citrus fruit and quarter them. Set a sieve over a bowl. Squeeze the juice from the fruit, using the sieve to catch the pips. Discard the pips. Pop the squeezed fruit into the bowl with the juice. Add the salt and chosen spices. Mix well.

Pack the fruit into sterilized jars (see page 78). Pour the salty brine and spices over the top, dividing them as evenly between the jars as possible.

Press the fruit down—the brine should cover the fruit—but if not, top up with filtered or mineral water (not tap water, as it contains chemicals that inhibit the fermenting process).

Seal the jar with a lid. Leave in a cool, dark place to mature, shaking often and checking to ensure the fruit is always covered in brine. If it's not, make up a brine solution using 100ml filtered or mineral water mixed with 4g sea salt and top up the jars.

The limes will be ready in about 4 weeks but will keep for years—I've kept them for up to 5 years. Store in the fridge once opened and use within 3 months (although as long as your jar is clean and the fruit is fully covered in brine, they'll keep longer).

KOMBU-CHAI

Kombucha is a tangy, refreshing drink made with a "scoby," which stands for "Symbiotic Culture of Bacteria and Yeast" (see page 32). It's a fermented drink, helpful for creating a harmonious internal microbiome—your gut flora—which is pivotal to overall health. Here it has a spicy, Indian chai kick, to which you can then add optional fruit for an extra layer of flavor and a seasonal twist.

Makes 1 liter (4 x 250ml servings)

4 tablespoons whole black or
   oolong tea leaves or 4 tea bags
1 cinnamon stick
12 cloves
8 black peppercorns
1 star anise
5 crushed cardamom pods
grating of nutmeg (optional)
4 slices of fresh ginger
1 liter freshly boiled water
85g raw, unrefined caster or brown
   sugar, plus 1 tablespoon
1 kombucha scoby (see page 32)
4 tablespoons kombucha or raw
   apple cider vinegar
fruit, to flavor (see below)

SEASONAL FRUIT FLAVORS

Pears: slices from 1 ripe pear
Apples: slices from 1 apple
Plums: slices from 2 ripe plums
Apricots: 2 ripe apricots
Cranberries: 3–4 tablespoons fresh
or bottled cranberry juice (add
extra sugar, if needed, to counter
the fruit's tartness)

Brew the tea with the spices, ginger and boiled water and leave to steep for 1 hour or longer. Strain the liquid and whisk in the sugar until it dissolves. Pour into a large jar with the kombucha scoby and extra kombucha from a previous batch (or apple cider vinegar). Cover the jar with a piece of cloth or a thin, clean tea towel, secure with string or a rubber band and leave to ferment for 1–2 weeks. Taste after a week; it should be a little yeasty but also mildly tangy. The longer you ferment it, the more sour and less sweet it will taste.

Once brewed, strain the kombucha through a fine-mesh sieve lined with a cloth to catch the scoby. Store the scoby in a container at room temperature with 4 tablespoons of kombucha. It will keep for several weeks between brews.

Whisk in 1 tablespoon of sugar to the brewed kombucha—this will help create carbonation. Add your choice of fruit (if using), then pour into bottles. The fruit is optional but it gives the kombucha added sugar to feed off, further lending to carbonation.

Keep the bottled kombucha at room temperature for a day to kickstart the second fermentation, then store in the fridge for up to 6 weeks. The longer you leave it, the less sweet and tangier it will become.

A great gift for anyone who is feeling run-down as the yeasty drink will help replenish the gut flora with good bacteria.

GINGER BEER

Making ginger beer is surprisingly easy and extremely satisfying. It takes about a week to ferment, and 5 minutes' attention a day. Use organic ginger as you are leaving the skin on—this houses all the lovely bacteria and yeasts. Non-organic ginger is often treated, thus preventing fermentation. This spicy beer makes wonderful cocktails when mixed with vodka or rum!

Makes 1 liter

1 whole organic fresh ginger root (about 12cm long), unpeeled
6 teaspoons unrefined caster sugar, plus 175g
1 liter filtered or mineral water
seasonal fruit, herbs or spices

In a 500ml jar, mix 1 tablespoon grated ginger, 1 teaspoon sugar and 3 tablespoons water. Cover with a piece of cloth and leave to ferment in a cool, dark cool place for 24 hours, shaking it a couple of times. After 24 hours, stir in 1 tablespoon grated ginger, 1 teaspoon sugar and 2 tablespoons water. Repeat daily for 5 days; you should start to see it fizz a little. This is your "ginger bug."

On the sixth day, stir the 175g unrefined caster sugar in a jug with 1 liter of water. Add 4–6 tablespoons of the ginger bug, more or less, to taste. Taste it and see how gingery you like it. You can even add more fresh ginger, if it needs a stronger kick of ginger.

Cover with a piece of cloth, secure with a rubber band and store in a dark place. Stir once or twice daily and taste daily. It will continue to ferment and become less sweet. Once to your taste (usually about 3–4 days) strain through a muslin cloth or thin, clean tea towel, then pour into sterilized bottles.

Let the bottles sit at room temperature for 1–2 days, then refrigerate. You may need to "burp" your bottles once or twice by opening then resealing them. This will release the pressure and prevent your bottles from exploding. Once refrigerated, drink within 2 weeks.

TIP: *Store the remaining ginger bug in the fridge for up to 2 weeks between batches. Simply top up to reactivate when you want to make a new batch of ginger beer.*

MOROCCAN POMEGRANATE KEFIR

In Australia, sparkling shiraz wine is traditionally sipped over the Christmas period. This is my probiotic take on the tipple, infused with fragrant rose and other tastebud-tingling spices. It's a beautiful, celebratory, aromatic drink brimming with antioxidants and heart-healthy pomegranate, and it completely woos anyone who tries it.

Makes 1 liter (4 x 250ml servings)

1 liter pomegranate juice
2 tablespoons rose petals or
  1 tablespoon rose water
12 cardamom pods, crushed
2 star anise
2 cinnamon sticks
12 cloves
1 tablespoon freshly grated or
  julienned ginger
1 clementine, thinly sliced
3 tablespoons demerara sugar
2 tablespoons water kefir grains (see
  Tip on page 54)

Put the pomegranate juice, rose petals, cardamom, star anise, cinnamon sticks, cloves, ginger and clementine slices into a large saucepan. Simmer for 15 minutes.

Take off the heat and cool fully. Strain into a sterilized jar (see page 78,) discarding the rose petals, spices and clementine slices. Stir in the sugar and kefir grains. Cover with a piece of cloth. Secure with string or a rubber band. Leave to ferment for 2 days.

Strain the water kefir grains out using a plastic sieve or a metal sieve lined with a cloth (contact with metal can damage the grains). Pour into sterilized bottles and store in the fridge until ready to serve. The drink will keep for 2 weeks, but will become dryer and less sweet as time goes by. Check the bottles every so often and release any building gases as the drink will continue to ferment in the fridge.

Store the kefir grains to use again at a later stage (see Tip on page 54).

Giving this drink along with some authentic Moroccan tea glasses makes a lovely package. Look out in charity and vintage shops for this gorgeous glassware—you'll be surprised what you can find!

ROSÉ KEFIR

This is a brilliant alternative to wine, with a similar vibe to rosé wine in taste and appearance. It's a beautiful offering that will be especially appreciated during detox January or sober October.

Makes 1 liter

1 liter filtered or mineral water
3 tablespoons golden caster sugar
2 tablespoons water kefir grains
  (see Tip on page 54)
2 prunes
1 tablespoon dried rosebuds
  or petals

Stir the sugar into the water in a 1.5 liter jar until dissolved. Add the kefir grains and prunes. Place the rosebuds or petals into a 15cm square piece of cheesecloth and secure with string to make a parcel. Add to the jar, then cover with a clean piece of cheesecloth.

Ferment at room temperature for 2 days or until fizzy, then chill before drinking. It will keep in the fridge for up to 2 weeks. Open the bottle every few days to "burp" and release the built-up gasses.

TURKISH COFFEE KOMBUCHA

This coffee kombucha packs an energy-and-wellbeing punch in one. Perfect for any coffee lover.

Makes 1 liter (4 x 250ml servings)

1 liter freshly brewed strong black
  coffee, brewed with 1 teaspoon
  freshly ground cardamom pods*
85g raw, unrefined caster sugar
1 kombucha scoby

*alternatively, put the cardamom in
  a square of cheesecloth to make a
  spice bag and add it along with the
  coffee and sugar.

Add the brewed cardamom coffee and sugar to a sterilized 1.5 liter glass jar (see page 78). Stir, then add the kombucha scoby—you can use one previously used for Kombuchai (see page 48).

Cover the jar with a piece of cloth or a thin, clean tea towel. Secure with string or a rubber band and leave to ferment for about 3 days, checking after 2 days and bottling after 4–5 days at the most. You're aiming for a flavor that's a little yeasty but also a little tangy. The longer you ferment it, the more sour and less sweet it will taste.

Store in the fridge for up to 3 weeks and store the scoby in a container at room temperature with 4 tablespoons coffee kombucha. It will keep for 4 weeks between brews.

CREAM SODA KEFIR

Naomi Devlin who teaches seasonal nutrition (and so much more) at River Cottage inspired and in part created this lovely recipe. It's brilliant if you're trying to wean teens off sugar-laden fizzy drinks, this might just do the trick. My 12-year-old son and his friends love it. I tend to bring it round as a gift for friends who have children. It's also lovely served at children's parties or family picnics.

Makes 1 liter

1 liter filtered or mineral water
3 tablespoons golden caster sugar
1–2 teaspoons licorice powder or
  1 licorice root, bashed
2 tablespoons water kefir grains
  (see Tip below)
2 unsulphured dried apricots
½ vanilla pod

VARIATION

Use a few fresh pineapple slices or 1 tablespoon pineapple powder (just dehydrated and ground pineapple flesh) in place of the dried apricots.

Stir the water, sugar and licorice powder until dissolved. Pour into a glass jar. Add the kefir grains, dried apricots, vanilla and licorice root (if using in place of powder). Cover with a cloth. Leave at room temperature (18–22°C/64–72°F) to ferment for 2 days, or until you're happy with the flavor—I like it to have a hint of tanginess while retaining a bit of sweetness, too—typically 2 days' fermenting does the trick, but you can brew for less time or longer. Strain out the kefir grains, apricots, vanilla and licorice root (if using).

Save the kefir grains for future brews—see tip below.

Bottle the strained cream soda kefir. Secure the lids on the bottle, but be mindful that carbonation will start to build up in the bottle, so you may need to burp it.

Refrigerate until ready to use. It will keep for 2 weeks, but the sugars will continue to ferment, so the drink will become less sweet the longer you leave it.

TIP: *Kefir grains are easily available to buy online. Once you've used them, can reuse the grains straight away or you can store them in the fridge. Simply strain out any other ingredients, rinse and spoon into a small jam jar and cover with a mix of 100ml water and 1 teaspoon sugar. Secure with a lid and store for 2 weeks. If you need to store them longer, simply pour off the water and top with a fresh batch of sweetened water.*

PICKLE

My pantry is never without an array of pickles, from Chinese-spiced plum pickles to sharp traditional Polish-style gherkins. A jar of pickles can completely transform a meal, or indeed, you can treat a good pickle, like my smoked beetroot pickles, as the star of the show—I love serving them with toasted walnuts either as a starter or at the end of a meal.

There are various methods for making pickles, but most fall under the umbrellas of infusing (you infuse the fruits or veggies in a vinegar brine) or fermenting, which typically uses a salt brine in place of the vinegar. Some pickles use a combination of the two.

For salt brining you need to mix in 4g sea salt for every 100ml water. Pack your veggies into sterilized jars (see page 78). Weigh up how much water you need to cover the veg. Add the correct ratio of salt. Stir to dissolve. Tuck some herbs or spices into the jars with your veggies. Pour the brine over and seal. Ferment at room temperature for 1–2 weeks, or longer—they'll keep for up to 2 months out of the fridge. Then refrigerate (for 6 months or more) until ready to eat.

For vinegar-based pickles, they could be as simple as just pouring cold vinegar over the veggies and leaving them to soften in a sealed jar for as long or as little as you like. Acidity of the vinegar is key. You want minimum 5 percent (which is typical for apple cider vinegar) or, ideally, 6 percent which is what you get with wine vinegars.

SMOKED BEETROOT PICKLE

Smoking root veg is by far one of the fastest and most exciting ways to cook them and it's a brilliant way of adding a wonderful layer of flavor to beetroot pickles, giving a marvelously modern twist.

Makes 4–5 x 300g jars

oak or apple wood chips
1kg beetroot
10 black peppercorns
5 cardamom pods, bruised
5 bay leaves
pinch of chili flakes
750ml red wine vinegar
100g maple syrup or clear honey
½ teaspoon sea salt

First, smoke the beetroot (or see Tip below). Add a 1cm layer of wood chips to the base of a cast-iron pot (that you don't mind charring on the inside). Set a rack inside the pot, such as a cooling rack, and put the beetroot on top of the rack. The smaller the beetroot, the faster and more evenly they will smoke.

Place over a high heat, ensuring you have good ventilation. Once the wood chips start smouldering secure the lid and leave to smoke for 15 minutes, or until the beetroot is softened. Add more wood chips if needed. You can also take off the heat and leave for several hours or overnight, if needed. Leave to cool, then remove the skin— it should come off easily by just rubbing it off with your fingers.

Next, make the pickling vinegar. Put the remaining ingredients in a saucepan and bring just to the boil. Cut the beetroot into bite-sized chunks (or leave whole if you're using baby beetroot).

Pack the beetroot into sterilized jars (see page 78). Top with the hot vinegar and seal. Store in a cool, dry place for at least 2 weeks before eating. They'll easily store for up to 1 year.

TIP: *There is an easier way to add a smoky edge without having to smoke the beetroot. Roast the beetroot for 45 minutes to 1 hour in an oven at 200°C/392°F until just tender. Follow the method above, but use chipotle chili and smoked sea salt instead of regular chili flakes and sea salt. Alternatively, if you can find oak-smoked water, add 1-2 teaspoons to the pickle towards the end of cooking. The depth of flavor won't be as great, but you'll get a nod in the right direction. For extra-smoky pickles, go the whole hog by smoking your beets and pairing them with chipotle chilies (smoked jalepeños) and smoked salt.*

POLISH DILL PICKLES

When we spent Christmas in Australia with my best friend, a fellow-pickler, she and my son made these gorgeous Polish-style pickles using the most delicious cucumbers from a local farm where we'd bought the rest of our Christmas dinner veg. They make a brilliant gift for a summer barbecue. These pickles are bottle processed, which is effectively a way of pasteurizing the contents of a jar giving it a longer shelf life. I can be applied to pickles, jams and more.

Makes 2 x 1kg jars

1kg small cucumbers
2 garlic cloves per jar, peeled and
   halved
3–4 black peppercorns per jar
2 sprigs dill per jar
1 liter filtered or mineral water
350ml white wine vinegar
100g sea salt

Sterilize 2 x 1kg screw band preserving jars (see page 78). Wash the cucumbers thoroughly. Nestle the cucumbers, halving them if necessary, into the jars with the garlic, peppercorns and dill.

Warm the water, vinegar and salt until it just comes to the boil and the salt has fully dissolved. Pour into the jars to within 1cm of the top. Secure the lids then turn by a half turn to loosen slightly—this will allow the steam to escape but allow no air in.

To bottle process the pickles, gently sit the jars in a tea towel-lined stockpot or a saucepan large enough to fully cover with water. Ensure they're not touching and are secure so they don't rattle in the pan—use wadded-up newspaper or extra cloth to protect them. Pour in enough simmering (38°C/100°F) water to cover the jars by 2–3cm. Let the water reach 88°C/190°F, cover and simmer for 20 minutes.

If you don't have a large enough pan, you can bottle process in an oven. Preheat the oven to 150°C/302°F. Line a deep roasting tray with a folded tea towel, stand the jars 5cm apart on top and fill the tray 3cm deep with water. Heat in the oven for 1 hour.

Take off the heat, or remove from the oven, and leave the jars in the water for 15 minutes. Carefully remove the jars and use a tea towel to fully fasten the lids. Leave undisturbed for 24 hours until completely cool. Check the seal by removing the screw-bands and carefully lifting the jar up by the lid. If it's well sealed the lid will remain firmly on. Re-fasten the lid and store, or if it comes away either reprocess and retest once fully cool, or eat straight away. Store in a cool, dry place for up to 1 year. Refrigerate once opened for 6 weeks.

QUICK PICKLED ONIONS

These tangy and crisp pickled onions are ready in 30 minutes. Perfect with sausages or burgers on summer barbecues, dished up on a cheeseboard, as a garnish for tacos or even a Sunday roast pork.

Makes 2 x 270ml jars

2 medium red onions, 200–250g
weight total
250ml filtered or mineral water
250ml apple cider vinegar, sherry
vinegar or white wine vinegar
3 tablespoons maple syrup or clear
honey
1 teaspoon sea salt
pinch of chili flakes

Pack the onions into two sterilized jars. In a small saucepan, combine the water, vinegars, maple syrup, salt and chili flakes. Bring the mixture to a gentle simmer over a medium heat, then, with the jars in the sink to catch any splashes, carefully pour the hot vinegar over the onions.

Use a spoon to press the onions down into the vinegar and pop any air bubbles in the jar. Leave to cool to room temperature for 20–30 minutes, at which point they should be ready to serve.

Cover and refrigerate any leftovers for later. They are best consumed within 3 days, but will keep for 2–3 weeks in the fridge.

KOMBUCHA-PICKLED PEARS

These gorgeous pickles are a great way of using up kombucha that has gone a little too tangy.

Makes 2 x 340g jar

2 pears, peeled, sliced and cored
a few slices of fresh ginger
2 star anise or 1 cinnamon stick,
halved
250ml kombucha

Place the pears in a sterilized jar (see page 78) with the spices. Pour over the kombucha to cover. Secure with a lid and store in the fridge until ready to eat. If the pears are fairly ripe they'll be nicely infused in 1–2 days. If they're more firm, leave at room temperature for 1–2 weeks until they're pickled to your liking. The pears will go soft after a month, so these are more quick pickles than long-life ones.

SANCHIA'S PICKLED GINGER

My introduction to Sanchia was via gifts she'd given one of my friends. Her amazing kimchi was laid on the table when we were having a cheese and pickle fest one afternoon. Another occasion involved a fridge forage for a quickly cobbled together meal and that's when I tried Sanchia's amazing pickled ginger. It had been maturing in my friend's fridge for some time (years, possibly), but it made an impression. It has all the familiar pickled ginger flavors and look, but it's so much better than anything you can buy. As with all homemade goodies, you're making it for quality and taste, not for commercial gain. Also, Sanchia has an incredible food flair and is an amazing cook, which is why I couldn't resist begging for her recipe. Thanks, Sanch!

**Makes 1 x 500g jar
(or 2 x 250g jars)**

250g root ginger (look for younger ginger, which will be less fibrous and easier to slice finely, rather than a super gnarled old root!)
2 teaspoons coarse sea salt
250ml rice vinegar (you need this for the pink color reaction, but you could use cider vinegar here too if you aren't looking for pink)
170g clear honey (something light colored rather than treacly)
100ml raw cider vinegar

OPTIONAL INGREDIENTS TO ADD

1 teaspoon dulse or other dried seaweed
1 teaspoon umeboshi plum purée
a few red shiso leaves (these will also color the ginger)

Peel and very finely slice the ginger. You want it to be as thin as possible. Sprinkle the sea salt over the ginger and leave for about 20 minutes. In the meantime, sterilize 1–2 jars (see page 78).

Gently heat the rice vinegar and honey. Add the dulse/umeboshi/shiso leaves to the vinegar (if using any or all of them). Add the ginger and remove from the heat.

Pack immediately into a large jar or two smaller jars and top up with the raw vinegar, then seal.

The ginger will be ready in about a week, but will soften and intensify a little when left longer. Store it in the fridge and use in stir-fries, sushi, broth or miso soup, or just as a pick-me-up. The ginger pickling liquid can be used to dress vegetables and salads and soups, or as a condiment—don't throw it away!

Give a batch of this pickle to a cheese lover along with a block of their favorite cheese.

BEER PICKLE

This is a fun way of incorporating beer into a pickle. A malty amber ale is ideal but you can use any favorite beer or, of course, choose the top tipple of the friend who'll receive this lovely treat.

**Makes 1 x 1.5 liter jar
(or 3 x 500ml jars)**

1 head cauliflower (or 1kg shallots
   or pickling onions)
400ml red ale (or any malty beer)
400ml water
400ml white wine vinegar or malt
   vinegar
3 tablespoons sea salt
1 teaspoon honey
1 teaspoon coriander seeds
1 teaspoon mustard seeds
1 teaspoon fennel seeds
1 teaspoon nigella seeds (optional)
1 chili, fresh or dried (chipotle chili is
   delicious here)
3 bay leaves
3 garlic cloves, peeled and scored
   with a cross at the end (to draw in
   more flavor)

Break or cut the cauliflower into bite-sized florets. (Use the cauliflower leaves to make Classic Sauerkraut on page 34, swapping them out for the cabbage).

Place the beer and water into a large saucepan. Boil rapidly for 5 minutes to burn off some of the alcohol. Add the vinegar, salt and honey to the pan and boil rapidly for 5 minutes.

Toast the coriander, mustard, fennel and nigella seeds (if using) in a dry frying pan. Add to the vinegar mix. Simmer for 10 minutes. Taste and adjust the seasoning if necessary, adding a bit more honey if it's too tangy.

Add the cauliflower florets. Cook for 2–3 minutes, just enough to just soften. Spoon the cauliflower into the jar(s). Tuck the chili, bay leaves and garlic in and among the cauliflower florets.

Pour in the hot vinegar mix. Seal the lids on the jar(s). Leave to mature for at least 24 hours in a cool, dark place before eating. Refrigerate and eat within 6 weeks of opening.

TIP: *Beyond a Ploughman's, this pickle is delicious served in a salad with leftover roast lamb, Puy lentils, watercress and hints of fresh orange.*

HOISIN PLUMS

You can apply this pickling brine to pretty much any damsons or cherries, or wild plums too. I typically make it with Victorian plums or wild cherry plums. If you're using firmer, wild fruit like wild cherry plums, allow the pickle to mature for longer, which will help soften the fruit over time. Or if you want to eat the pickle sooner, you can roast the plums first or boil them in the vinegar mixture until they start to soften, then pack into the jar to mature further.

Makes 1 x 340ml jar

200g plums
150ml raw apple cider or red wine
   vinegar
50ml water
¼ teaspoon sea salt
2 tablespoons maple syrup, sugar
   (any kind) or honey
1 star anise
1 teaspoon fennel seeds
8 Szechuan peppercorns
6 black peppercorns
6 cloves

Wash and dry the fruit. Halve or quarter the plums, depending on size—you want nice bite-sized chunks. Keep any smaller fruits whole. Pack the fruit into a sterilized jar (see page 78).

Warm the vinegar, water, salt, 1 tablespoon maple syrup and the spices for 5 minutes. Taste, adding more maple syrup to taste if necessary.

Pour the warm vinegar mix over the fruit until it comes right to the top of the jar. Seal with the lid. Give the jar a shake every day or so. Let the pickles mature for at least 3 months before eating. They'll keep for a year. Refrigerate once opened.

This pickle is a lovely accompaniment to soft, creamy goat's cheeses - especially ash-coated French cheeses, which you can offer up as a gift pairing for the pickle. Alternatively, you can pair it with Chinese-style pancakes and crispy duck.

MOROCCALILLI

I've tried lots of different piccalilli recipes in the past, and I really think there's none better than Pam Corbin's from the *River Cottage Preserves Handbook*. It's faultless and utterly delicious. It's also hugely flexible in terms of which summer veg you can tumble into it. I think it's a true celebration of late summer veg, and come winter, it's one of my favorite things to open up to bring back all those memories of long, lazy sunshine-filled days. My store cupboard's never without a jar.

Makes 3 x 340g jars

1kg vegetables, a mixture of at least 3 of the following: cauliflower or romanesco, green or runner beans, zucchini, squash, green or yellow tomatoes, small silver-skinned onions, peppers, nasturtium seed pods
50g fine sea salt
20g cornflour
10g ras el hanout
thumb of fresh ginger, peeled and finely grated
pinch of saffron
1 teaspoon cumin seeds
1 teaspoon coriander seeds
1 teaspoon fennel seeds
½ teaspoon turmeric
½ teaspoon ground cinnamon
600ml cider vinegar
150g golden caster sugar
50g honey

Cut the vegetables into small, even, bite-sized pieces. Place in a large bowl and sprinkle with the salt. Mix well, cover the bowl with a tea towel and leave in a cool place for 24 hours, then rinse the veg with ice-cold water and drain thoroughly.

Blend the cornflour, ras el hanout, ginger, saffron, cumin, coriander fennel, turmeric and cinnamon to a smooth paste with a little of the vinegar. Put the rest of the vinegar into a saucepan with the sugar and honey, and bring to the boil. Spoon a little of the hot vinegar over the blended spice paste, stir well, then tip the spice mixture into the pan. Bring gently to the boil. Boil for 3–4 minutes to allow the spices to release their flavors into the thickening sauce.

Remove the pan from the heat and carefully fold the well-drained vegetables into the hot, spicy vinegar. Pack the pickle into warm, sterilized jars (see page 78) and seal immediately with vinegar-proof lids. Leave (if you can) for 4–6 weeks before opening. Use within 1 year.

LIME PICKLE

This is a brilliant and relatively easy mildly fermented lime pickle. Any lover of Indian food will go bonkers for it, but it's also brilliant for any cook who wants a fun ingredient to play with as the pickle is just as gorgeous in stews (think lamb or even a veggie stew) or used to jazz up salads and roasted vegetables, or served alongside roasted meat.

Makes 1 x 500g or 2 x 250g jars

500g limes
85g salt
2 teaspoons cumin seeds
2 teaspoons fennel seeds
2 teaspoons coriander seeds
1 teaspoon fenugreek seeds
2 teaspoons mustard seeds
100ml rapeseed oil
1 tablespoon garam masala
½ teaspoon chili powder
1 teaspoon nigella seeds
85g jaggery or brown sugar

Cut each lime into eights. Add to a large bowl. Massage the salt into the lime. Cover and leave at room temperature to ferment overnight.

Set a frying pan over a medium heat. Add the cumin, fennel, coriander, mustard and fenugreek seeds. Lightly toast until just fragrant. Remove from the heat and grind to a powder in a coffee grinder or a pestle and mortar.

Gently heat the oil in a frying pan until just hot. Remove from the heat. Add all the ground spices as well as the garam masala, chili powder and nigella seeds. Stir in the brown sugar.

Cool the spiced oil thoroughly and add the fermented lime and the salty brine. Mix well and pack into sterilized jars (see page 78).

Shake the jar(s) well and keep in the sun for a week. Leave to mature for another week before eating. The pickle will keep for up to 6 months at room temperature. Once opened, store in the fridge and consume within 2 weeks.

MANGO CHUTNEY

I once had the pleasure of making mango chutney with Geeta Samtani, who has created a gorgeous brand of Indian pickles and preserves inspired by family recipes. Her mango chutney is second to none and this recipe is inspired by hers. Pictured on page 68 with Lime Pickle.

Makes 2 x 250g jars

2 ripe mangos yielding about 500g
   flesh (once the stone and skin are
   removed)
200ml white wine vinegar or apple
   cider vinegar
300g golden caster sugar
2 tablespoons freshly grated ginger
½ teaspoon sea salt
4 garlic cloves, peeled and finely
   chopped
½ teaspoon cumin seeds
½ teaspoon mixed spice
½ teaspoon nigella seeds (optional)
8 black peppercorns, ground
6 cardamom pods, ground
4 whole cloves
pinch of chili powder, more or less,
   to taste

Peel, stone and finely dice the mangos. Place the flesh in a large saucepan with the vinegar and sugar.

Bring to the boil and simmer for about 5 minutes, or until the fruit is just soft, stirring occasionally.

Add the remaining ingredients and simmer for a further 20 minutes. The chutney will thicken slightly on cooling.

Spoon into sterilized jars (see page 78), seal, label and mature for 1 week before eating. It will keep at room temperature for up to 1 year. Store in the refrigerator once opened and eat within 1 month.

Make a batch of Mango Chutney along with some Lime Pickle and give both to a curry loving friend or family member.

MY GRANNY'S BREAD & BUTTER PICKLES

These pickles have been a firm favorite since childhood when my granny used to make them. To give them a one-year shelf life, you can "bottle" process them as with the dill pickles (see page 60). Typically you'd eat them with bread and butter (like a basic ploughmans, though this can be quite a gourmet one if you use nice bread and butter, along with homemade pickles!). They're also lovely with burgers and sausages, in any sandwich or on a cheeseboard, or just as a snack.

Makes 500ml jar

400g firm, small cucumbers, cut into
   1cm-thick slices
1 small onion, cut into 1cm-thick
   slices
2 tablespoons sea salt
300ml apple cider vinegar
200ml filtered or mineral water
150g golden caster sugar
2 tablespoons yellow or brown
   mustard seeds
¼ teaspoon celery seeds
1–2 cloves

Put the cucumbers, onion and salt in a sieve set over a bowl, and cover with ice and something to weigh it down. Leave to stand for 1–2 hours in the fridge, then drain well and rinse under ice cold water. (This process helps the pickle stay crunchy—you can also add a grape leaf to the jar with the pickles to help keep them crisp.)

Put the vinegar, water, sugar, mustard and celery seeds and cloves in a saucepan over a medium heat. Bring to the boil and simmer for 5 minutes. Remove from the heat and leave to cool to room temperature.

Pack the cucumber and onion mixture in the jar, pour over the hot brine, cover and seal. Keep at room temperature for up to 6 months. You can keep for longer, but the pickles will start to soften quite a bit after this time. Refrigerate once opened and eat within 6 weeks.

"TINNED" TOMATOES

An absolutely must-have store cupboard staple, in my mind, are tinned tomatoes. They're the base for so many meals, and when summer throws you a glut of tomatoes I can think of few better ways to preserve them. The "tin" in this instance is a glass jar designed especially for a DIY version of pressure cooking, also known as bottling. My granny always preserved her tomatoes this way. It seems to have gone out of fashion a bit, but it's a technique well worth reviving as it's a brilliant way to preserve with minimal sugar and salt.

Makes 3 x 500g jars

1kg cherry tomatoes like San
  Marzano
1½ teaspoons sea salt
1½ tablespoons cider vinegar
a few sprigs of fresh thyme or
  bay leaves

Sterilize 3 screw band preserving jars or clip jars with rubber seals (see page 78).

Bring a saucepan of water to the boil. Make a small cross-shaped cut on the top of each tomato, about 5mm deep. Add the tomatoes to the boiling water for 30 seconds, drain and plunge into very cold water to prevent further cooking. Drain again and peel the skins from the tomatoes starting at the top where you made the small cuts.

Add ½ teaspoon sea salt and ½ tablespoon cider vinegar to each jar. Gently nestle the tomatoes into the jars, being careful not to crush them. Tuck a few sprigs of thyme of a bay leaf into each jar. Pour enough boiling water over the tomatoes to fully cover, leaving a 1.5cm space. Gently jostle the jars or use the handle of a spoon to release any air bubbles. Wipe the rims clean. Place the lids on top. Give the jar a sharp knock to remove any trapped air before screwing the lid on tightly, then loosen by half a turn.

Bottle process the jars by following the method on page 60, simmering for 40 minutes. Once you're happy they're sealed properly store in a cool, dry place for up to 1 year.

APPLE PICKLE

I tried making these pickles both with cider vinegar and a salt brine and the pickles resulting from the latter were, by far, my favorite. The apple flavor really comes through and you get these wonderful tender, lightly pickled apple rings, which are brilliant with roast pork or on toasted, bubbling melted cheese-topped toast. They're also brilliant in sandwiches or salads, or served alongside quiche or any savory tart.

The recipe below is for one jar so you can quickly bundle a few apples into a jar if you're in search of a last-minute gift you can whip up before you dash out the door, but it scales up easily.

Makes enough for 1 x 500g jar

2–3 eating apples
1 cinnamon stick and/or 1 star anise
a few slices of fresh ginger
1 fresh or dried bay leaf
375ml water
15g sea salt

If you have an apple corer, remove the core of your apples. If not, just leave it. Cut the apple horizontally into ½–1cm-thick slices—don't cut them too thinly or they'll get too soft. Tuck the cinnamon and/or star anise, ginger and bay leaf into a sterilized jar (see page 78) with the apple slices. You can use the tops and bottoms of the apples, too, if you like—having one of the apple tops capping the stack looks rather pretty.

Stir the water with the salt until the salt has fully dissolved. Pour over the apples. Seal the jar. Leave to ferment for a week before eating.

To give this as a larger gift, double or triple the quantities and combine in a larger mason jar, adding a label with some of the suggested uses from the introduction to make it even more special.

JAM

Waking up to a lovely jar of something homemade to spread on toast, dollop over porridge or swirl through yogurt is a delight, especially if there's a story attached to it ... berries picked from a summer garden, apples foraged in the autumn.

This chapter is packed with some of my favorite spreads, mostly jams, some amazing marmalades, a few healthier fruit butters, and a nourishing chocolate spread that my son has loved (even over the sugar-laden commercial varieties) for years. The key with these recipes—in particular the jams and fruit butters—is to remove excess moisture to preserve the ingredients and therefore create spreads that have a longer shelf life than other produce.

Some of the jam recipes contain classic, long shelf-life amounts of sugar—this is traditionally equal sugar to weight of fruit which can be quite a large quantity—but on the next page there are tips on how to trim this right back to lower the sugar content. Personally, I quite like a sweet, glossy jam made traditionally, but I eat it as a treat, not often. Also when they contain more sugar, you tend to eat less because it's so sweet.

Here I've given you the option of both so you can make it to your liking. Just be aware, trimming back the sugar decreases the shelf-life slightly, but for gifts that will be consumed quickly this gives more flexibility. You can play around with different types of sugar but my favorite is always raw, organic, golden caster sugar or local honey.

A FEW BASICS

How to sterilize jars
Preheat the oven to 180°C/356°F. Wash the jars and lids thoroughly with hot soapy water. Put the jars in the oven for 10 minutes. Carefully place the lids in boiling water for the same amount of time. When they're done, slide them into the oven, with the top of the lid facing upwards, for about 2–3 minutes until just dry. Take the jars and lids out of the oven and fill them while they're still hot.

How to test setting point
Saucer test: Place a saucer in the fridge or freezer before you start. Drop a little jam onto the cold saucer. Allow to cool for 1 minute, then push gently with your fingertip. If the jam crinkles, setting point has been reached. This is my go-to method (and the easiest) to test setting point.

Temperature test: Place a preserving thermometer in the jam when it has reached the boil. Once it reaches 104.5°C/220°F setting point will have been reached. Pectin-rich fruits (gooseberries, currants, apples, damsons, quince and citrus) will set a degree or two lower.

Full sugar jam vs. fridge jam
Most jam is made with equal amounts of sugar and fruit. If you're watching how much sugar you consume you can lower the amount of sugar by up to 50 percent. Simply halve the amount of sugar listed in the ingredients and keep the fruit the same. The resulting jam will need to be stored in the fridge and it won't have the glossy shine of full-sugar jam, but it will taste delicious nonetheless.

How to scale up or down—how to know what your yield is going to be
You can scale any of these recipes up or down. If you're not sure how many jars you'll need and what sizes, the best way to calculate this is to add up the total weight of the ingredients, divide this number by three and multiply it by two as cooking the fruit down for jam tends to reduce the weight by a third. Alternatively, pour your jam into a measuring jug (ideally one with a lip to help you pour your jam into the jars) and you'll see the final volume to help you know which jars and how many to use.

Tips on jars/lids/wax seals
By all means, reuse your old jam jars. The lids are the only thing you'll need to replace from time to time as they have a little wax seal on the inner rim that will deteriorate after 2–3 uses. I normally place a little dot with a permanent marker on my lids each time I use them so I can keep tabs. Once I've used a lid twice, I replace it for jams or anything that needs to be heat-sealed, but you can reuse these lids for jars storing dried foods, ferments or any other preserve that doesn't need to be heat-sealed airtight.

Processing fruit butters for storage
Place hot fruit butter in hot sterilized jars (see above), leaving 0.5cm headspace. Cover with hot sterilized lids and rings. Bottle process following the method on page 60, check the seal and store in a cool, dry, dark place for up to a year. If the seal does not hold, store in the fridge and eat within 2 weeks.

ONE-PUNNET STRAWBERRY JAM

I was keen to illustrate how simple it is to make homemade jam, but also to show that you don't need to spend a whole day in the kitchen doing it, nor do you need to make vats of the stuff.

Most of the jam I make is in small batches, using produce I've gathered from my allotment, foraged from the hedgerows, or produce lingering in my fridge or fruit bowl that needs to be used up. So turn to this recipe in those moments when you have a handful of produce you want to celebrate or share as a gift for family or friends.

Makes 1 x 200–250g jar

225g fresh strawberries (or any other seasonal fruit)
1 lemon
about 200g golden caster sugar

Hull the strawberries. Add the strawberries to a saucepan with the zest from the lemon. Use your hands, a fork or a potato masher to crush the strawberries. Place over a medium heat and cook the strawberries for about 5 minutes, or until they start to break down a little and begin to release their juices.

Take off the heat and add the lemon juice. Weigh the berries and juice. Add an equal amount of sugar. Mix it through until the sugar has fully dissolved.

Place the mixture back over a medium–high heat and bring to the boil. Cook for 3–5 minutes, or until the jam has thickened to the point where it coats the back of a spoon or passes the saucer test (see opposite). Another visual sign it has set is that you will be able to drag the spoon across the bottom of the pan and see the base for a moment before the jam comes back together.

If the jam separates and doesn't come back together, your jam is overset but this is easy to remedy. Just add a splash or two of water and bring back up to the boil until the dragging spoon test works to the point where the jam will come apart for a moment but then come back together.

ROASTED RASPBERRY JAM

This evolved from an original Elizabeth David recipe. Roasting the fruit intensifies the flavor and it's an easy, hands-off method that I've used with blueberries and apples, too, with success.

Makes about 1.5kg

1kg raspberries
zest of 1 lemon
950g granulated sugar

Preheat the oven to 200°C/392°F. Combine the raspberries and lemon zest on a baking tray, and put the sugar on a separate baking tray. Put both trays in the oven, raspberries on the top shelf and the sugar below, for 20–30 minutes. The raspberries should release a fair amount of juice and look substantially softened, while the sugar should start to melt a little around the edges.

While they are still hot, mix the berries through the sugar and stir thoroughly to break them up into a jammy consistency. Spoon or pour into warm, sterilized jam jars (see page 78), filling right to the top. Seal immediately. Store in a cool, dry place for up to 1 year.

MULLED FIG JAM

This gorgeous jam is as good on toast as it is paired with cheese or meat like smoked duck, game or goose. It's also a delicious addition to Christmas puddings, or served with yogurt and toasted nuts.

Makes 3–4 x 200g jars

500g ripe figs, tough tips removed
  and chopped to a paste
zest and juice of 1 orange
250ml red wine
1 cinnamon stick
6 cloves
4 bruised cardamom pods
3 black peppercorns
3 slices fresh ginger
500g golden caster sugar

Place the chopped figs, orange zest and juice, red wine and 250ml water into a heavy-based saucepan or jam pan. Put the spices and ginger into a square of cheesecloth and tie into a secure bundle, then add to the pan. Simmer over medium heat for 30 minutes, or until the figs have started to break down and soften. Take off the heat, remove the spice bag (squeezing it to extract as much flavor and liquid as possible), and stir in the sugar until dissolved.

Return to the heat and bring back to the boil for 5 minutes, or until the mixture thickens into a jammy consistency. It will thicken rather than reach a setting point, so bear this in mind when determining the desired consistency.

When ready, take off the heat, remove any scum and leave to sit for 5 minutes. Ladle into warm, dry sterilized jars (see page 78) and seal.

The jam will keep for up to 1 year unopened. Once opened, refrigerate and consume within 4 weeks.

VICTORIAN APPLE JAM

I first came across apple jam when I was asked to host some Victorian preserving workshops in a walled garden with an orchard near my house. I did lots of research on Victorian recipes and apple jam was pretty mainstream back then. I'm not sure why it's not more readily available in the shops now but it certainly should be. On warm, buttered toast, this is like a breakfast version of apple crumble or apple pie. I love it. You can also use the jam as a glaze for ham.

Makes 4–5 x 200g jars

500g apples
1 cinnamon stick
juice of 1 lemon
900g–1kg golden caster sugar

VARIATION

In place of the cinnamon use:
seeds from 8 cardamom pods,
    crushed, and 2 tablespoons
    freshly grated ginger
1 teaspoon ground chai blend,
    available in Indian supermarkets
    and online (or make your own by
    grinding ½ cinnamon stick,
    4 black peppercorns, 1 star anise,
    seeds from 3 cardamom pods
    and 6 cloves)

Peel and coarsely grate the apples, discarding the cores.

Add the apple to a heavy-based saucepan along with the cinnamon and 750ml water. Simmer for 20 minutes or until the flesh is mashably tender—top up with water during cooking if it starts to dry out. The water should reduce down to about 500ml, giving you equal weight of apples and water.

Remove the cinnamon stick and add the lemon juice. Measure the mixture and add an equal weight of sugar. Return to the pan, off the heat, and stir until the sugar has fully dissolved.

When the sugar has dissolved, set the pan over medium-high heat and bring up to the boil until it's set. See tips on how to test setting point (page 78). Pour into sterilized jars while the jam is still hot. Seal straight away. The jam will keep for up to 1 year. Refrigerate once opened and eat within a month.

MARROW MARMALADE

I've made all manner of marmalade variations. When I teach preserving courses at River Cottage Cookery School I let the students sample a host of different flavors, and this one is always the most popular, beating both the classic Dundee Seville marmalade and my popular blood orange and rhubarb marmalade. It's a brilliant way of shifting a marrow (or zucchini) glut. I love making these with yellow zucchini, keeping the skin on for added texture and color.

Makes 4–5 x 340g jars

1kg marrows or zucchini, peeled
   (unless the zucchini are lovely and
   yellow) and coarsely grated
juice and zest of 4 lemons
1kg caster sugar
large thumb of ginger, peeled and
   finely diced or grated
1 tablespoon fennel blossom or
   a pinch of saffron (optional)

Set a large preserving or heavy-based saucepan (large enough to hold 2 liters) over a medium heat. Add the marrows or zucchini and the finely grated lemon zest (this has pectin in which will help your jam set). Cook for 5–10 minutes, stirring often, until the marrow softens and starts to release some juices.

Add the lemon juice. Weigh the mixture and add an equal amount of sugar. Return to the pan and stir, off the heat, until the sugar has fully dissolved.

Increase the heat. Once it reaches a full boil, boil rapidly for 20–30 minutes, or until setting point is reached (see page 78). You can see and hear the jam reach setting point, too, as it will turn from a really frothy, rapid bubble to a calmer, denser sticky pool. Add the ginger and fennel blossom or saffron (if using) just as the jam is reaching setting point. Sample as you add, adding more or less to taste. Adding the fennel at the final stage means you're not cooking out all its flavor—giving the marmalade a really fresh finish of fennel (but omit if you're not a fan of fennel, or swap with something else like cardamom).

Once set, remove from the heat. If there's any white frothy or scummy bits on the top you can just stir them back in—stirring in one direction. Spoon or pour into warm, sterilized jars (see page 78), filling right to the top. Seal immediately.

Store in a cool, dry place for up to 1 year.

BLOOD ORANGE & RHUBARB MARMALADE

This marmalade has a multitude of uses: spread on toasted sourdough with goat's curd cheese; mix with ginger, chili and a splash of soy sauce as a dip; mix with olive oil and orange juice to make a delicious dressing for celeriac or beetroot; or ripple through vanilla ice cream.

Makes 4–5 x 200g jars

500g blood oranges, scrubbed
500g rhubarb, thinly sliced
juice of 1 lemon
1.5kg golden granulated or
  demerara sugar

VARIATIONS

½ teaspoon orange blossom water
  (add right at the end of cooking)
spices such as cardamom,
  cinnamon or star anise (added
  to the cheesecloth bag)

Halve and juice the oranges. Then halve each halve so you have four pieces for each orange. Reserve the juice for later.

Use a sharp knife to slice the quartered peel into thin shreds. Add to a heavy-based saucepan or jam pan with 1.25 liters water. Set over medium-high heat and bring to the boil. Lower the heat a little and cook until the peel is soft enough to fully mash between your fingers. Top up with more water, if needed. You want to end up with an equal amount of peel to water.

Once the peel is fully tender, take off the heat. Check that you have about the same ratio of peel to water—pour off any excess water, if needed, or top up if it's too low. Add the rhubarb and reserved orange juice. Weigh all this up and add an equal amount of sugar.

Return to the pan and stir the sugar through, off the heat, until it's fully dissolved.

Place the marmalade back on the heat, bring it up to the boil and boil rapidly for about 15 minutes until setting point is reached (see page 78). Remove from the heat and leave to cool for 8–10 minutes, then stir gently to disperse any scum or skim it from the top. Pour into warm, sterilized jars (see page 78) and seal immediately. Use within 1 year.

Give a jar of marmalade along with a loaf of sourdough from your local bakery for the ultimate comfort gift.

AUSTRIAN PLUM BUTTER

Also known as *powidl*, this plum butter is often used as a filling for desserts in the Austrian kitchen, such as *Germknödel*, a sweet, thick yeast dumpling. It's just as stunning on buttery toast, slathered on cakes, paired with cheese or used in sauces for roast game. While ripe Victoria plums are ideal, I've also made it with tart and tangy wild plums, but a dollop of honey is needed for sharper fruits.

Makes 2 x 200g jars

800g ripe plums, halved and
  stoned
1 teaspoon ground cinnamon
2–3 tablespoons honey (depending
  on sweetness of plums)
½ vanilla pod (optional)

Preheat the oven to 200°C/392°F. Arrange the plums in a roasting tin and roast for 20 minutes, or until the plums have fully cooked down and look like a compote.

Scrape the mixture into a bowl or saucepan and blend with a stick blender, or transfer to a food-processor and blend until smooth. Press through a fine mesh sieve to remove the plum skins, giving you a smooth purée.

Mix in the cinnamon, honey and vanilla (if using). Spoon the mixture into a saucepan and cook until it's thick enough to coat the back of a spoon, about 5–10 minutes.

If you want a longer shelf life, bottle process following the method on page 60, simmering for 15 minutes. Once sealed properly it will keep at room temperature for 6 months.

Alternatively, store in a normal jam jar but keep it in the fridge and use within 2 weeks after opening.

QUINCE HONEY BUTTER

This is very similar to membrillo but it's easier to make and easier to use in many ways as it spreads nicely on toast and can also be swirled through yogurt or into puddings, custards, dolloped into tarts, woven into an apple crumble filling and more.

Makes 250g

450g quince
juice of 1 lemon
150g honey

VARIATIONS

1 star anise, added to the water and removed before puréeing, and 1 tablespoon freshly grated ginger added before puréeing and cooking down

1–2 teaspoons rose water added with the honey

Coarsely grate the quince—leave the skin on but discard the cores once you get to them.

Place the quince in a saucepan with the lemon juice. Pour in enough water to cover the quince by 5cm. Bring to the boil, then reduce the heat to low and let it simmer for 30 minutes, or until the quince are tender—test a bit of grated quince to see if you can fully mash it with the back of a spoon when laid on a chopping board. Top up with water if the mixture gets too dry—the fruit should be just covered with water throughout cooking.

Once the quince are soft, drain the water but save it. Purée the quince with a splash of the cooking water, trickling in more, little by little, until you have a smooth apple sauce-like purée.

Preheat your oven to 180°C/356°F. Stir the honey into the quince purée, then spoon the mixture into a baking dish, creating a layer 3–4cm deep (if it's thinner, decrease the cooking time, if it's thicker, bake for a little longer).

Bake in the center of the oven for 30–45 minutes, or until it has thickened and darkened in color, picking up a light ruby hue.

For a longer shelf life, follow the method on page 60 for bottle processing. Once sealed correctly it will keep at room temperature for 6 months.

Alternatively, store in a normal jam jar in the fridge and use within 2 weeks after opening.

LEMON CURD

Classic lemon curd is my favorite, but I also have a soft spot for passion fruit or blackcurrant curd. To make one of these variations, simply press the fresh fruit through a fine mesh sieve until you have 100g and use it in place of the lemon zest and juice.

Makes 2 x 150g jars

finely grated zest and juice
  of 2 lemons
50g butter
130g caster sugar
2 eggs, plus 2 egg yolks

Combine the lemon zest and juice with the butter and sugar in a small heatproof bowl. Rest the bowl over a small saucepan of gently simmering water, ensuring the bowl doesn't touch the water. Turn the heat down to low and whisk until the butter has melted.

Whisk the egg and egg yolk together and add to the lemon mixture. Gently cook, whisking regularly, until the curd thickens. This should take about 15 minutes. Spoon into a cooled sterilized jar (see page 78) and seal with a lid. Use within 4 weeks. Refrigerate once opened.

PEACH & LAVENDER BUTTER

This fresh summer peach and lavender combination is gorgeous at breakfast or as a dessert.

Makes about 500g

7 peaches, halved and stoned
2 sprigs fresh lavender
125ml maple syrup

Blend the peaches to a purée. Pass through a fine mesh sieve, scraping it so you get as much pulp through as possible.

Place the pulp into a heavy-based saucepan and bring to a gentle boil. Cook, stirring often, until reduced to a thick paste and reduce by about half. Add the lavender and the maple syrup and reduce until the butter is thick enough to coat the back of a spoon—you should also be able to see the bottom of the pan when you drag a spoon through the mix.

Bottle process as on page 60 or store in the fridge for up to 3 weeks, or in the freezer for up to a year.

HOMEMADE TAHINI

I always find it difficult to get through a bag of sesame seeds and I never seem to have enough tahini. My solution to these kitchen conundrums is to whip up my excess sesame seeds into homemade tahini, which is as (if not more) delicious than anything you can buy in the shops. It's also much cheaper if you make it yourself. However, because sesame seeds are so dinky, you need a coffee grinder or a very small food processor (or a strong arm and a big pestle and mortar) to make it. If you like the idea but don't have the kit, swap the sesame seeds for cashew nuts (or any other nut) and whip up a nut butter instead, which you can use as a direct swap for tahini in a recipe, too.

Makes 100g

100g sesame seeds
2–3 tablespoons olive oil,
    rapeseed oil or
    sunflower oil

In a food processor, blend the sesame seeds with the oil until you have a smooth paste. I usually start by blending the seeds on their own, adding the oil little by little until the paste is as smooth as I like it—I like it pretty smooth so end up using 3 tablespoons of oil, sometimes a little more!

You can toast the sesame seeds first, if you like. This will give you a darker tahini. I prefer keeping them raw, resulting in a lighter tahini.

Make up a little Middle Eastern food hamper by pairing a jar of this with the Home-grown Rose Harissa (page 133) and Persian Dried Limes (page 136).

CHOCOLATE HAZELNUT SPREAD

This is very similar to commercial chocolate hazelnut spreads, but when you make it yourself, you can use the best possible ingredients, making it even better, if not mildly healthier.

Makes 250g

200g hazelnuts
4 tablespoons raw cacao or cocoa
  powder
2 tablespoons olive oil or coconut
  oil
10 pitted dates
¼ teaspoon ground cinnamon
Seeds from ½ vanilla pod (optional)
2–4 tablespoons water
a pinch of sea salt

Preheat the oven to 180°C/356°F.

Spread the hazelnuts in a single layer on a baking sheet and toast in the oven for about 7–10 minutes, until they've browned a little and the skins are slightly blistered. Wrap them in a clean cloth and rub vigorously to remove as much loose skin as possible. (Some skin will cling to the nuts when you're done but that's okay.)

In a food processor, grind the hazelnuts until they form a paste. Add the cacao or cocoa, oil, dates, cinnamon and vanilla, if using. Continue processing, tricking in the water until the mixture is as smooth as you can get it—you might need to blend for a little while, or add a little more water, but you should end up with a nice spreadable mix. Add a little salt, to taste.

Scrape into a jar. It will keep at room temperature for up to 1 week or in the fridge for up to 2 weeks.

Make a personalized label with the recipient's name for any chocolate spread lover.

BAKE

Few gifts cheer me more than a parcel of homemade biscuits, sweet or breakfast treats—especially if they've been made by someone I love and even better if they taste amazing without being outrageously unhealthy. The following recipes are incredibly decadent and delicious, but don't contain unnecessary amounts of sugar. For the most part, I've opted for whole grain flours and have also tucked in protein-rich nuts or seasonal fruits. Where I've used plain white flour, I've done so because I tested the recipe with a whole grain option and felt it compromised the end result—but you can substitute a whole grain option if you'd prefer.

Many of the recipes are vegan, but the ones that aren't can be easily adapted by swapping honey for maple syrup, date syrup or molasses, butter for coconut oil, and any eggs can be replaced with aquafaba (chickpea water). For every egg you'll need 50g of whipped aquafaba.

CHESTNUT SNOWBALLS

A stunning way to celebrate wild chestnuts, if you can get your hands on some—I love gathering them from my local woods or on an autumnal foray in the park, but if you can't find wild chestnuts you can buy them or use vac-packed chestnuts.

Makes 12 biscuits

50g shelled, cooked chestnuts
2 tablespoons butter or coconut oil
2 tablespoons olive oil
2 tablespoons coconut sugar or
  icing sugar, plus 75g for dusting
4 tablespoons maple syrup
½ teaspoon ground cinnamon, plus
  1 teaspoon for dusting
a few gratings of fresh nutmeg
a pinch of sea salt
75g plain white
2 tablespoons chestnut flour

Finely chop or pulse the chestnuts in a food processor until they're as fine as you can get them. Add the butter and olive oil and pulse until combined. Add the sugar, maple syrup, cinnamon, nutmeg, salt and flour, and pulse until it all comes together into a dough that's soft but firm enough to work with, a bit like Play-Doh. If it's looking too dry, add a little water (1–3 tablespoons) to bring it together.

Chill the dough for 20 minutes in the freezer, or freeze to make the biscuits at a later date. I like to make batches of the dough during chestnut season and freeze it to cook at Christmas.

Preheat the oven to 180°C/356°F. Rub a large baking sheet with enough oil to light coat. Scoop the dough up by the tablespoon and roll into 12 smooth balls. Arrange on the baking sheet leaving 2–3cm between each biscuit. Bake 10 minutes, or until golden. Cool fully before removing from the tray.

Mix the remaining sugar with 1 teaspoon ground cinnamon and dust over the cooked biscuits to coat. Serve straight away or store in an airtight container for up 3 days.

Fill a glass jar full of the biscuits and secure the lid with either a decorative ribbon or a piece of pretty material. If you can get your hands on a chestnut leaf, it makes a lovely, relevant and earthy gift tag.

SICILIAN SHORTBREAD

I've always loved baking with olive oil in both cakes, muffins and biscuits as I think it lends a silky, melt-in-your mouth flavor you just can't get with butter, and these biscuits are even lighter and healthier with the use of white rye or buckwheat flour. The latter gives them a darker appearance, especially if you use coconut sugar, but they're utterly delicious nonetheless.

Makes 12 pieces

350g plain white flour
175g icing sugar or coconut sugar
¼ teaspoon sea salt
¼ teaspoon ground cinnamon
zest of 2 lemons
175g olive oil
4 tablespoons shelled pistachios,
  roughly chopped (optional)

VARIATION

For coffee walnut shortbread,
  swap the lemon and pistachios
  for 1 tablespoon finely ground
  coffee and 4 tablespoons roughly
  chopped walnuts

Preheat the oven to 160°C/320°F. Mix the flour, sugar, salt, cinnamon, lemon zest and chopped pistachios (if using) together in a large bowl. Stir in the olive oil in until everything comes together.

Smooth the dough across a 22cm square baking tray or one roughly of the same size, ideally one with a removable base—if you have a tin that's much larger you can portion it off by using a folded piece of foil. The dough should be no thicker than 2cm. Prick with a fork in rows about 3–4cm wide, leaving a 1–2cm space between each fork mark. You should end up with 12 pieces of shortbread.

Bake for 20 minutes, or until just golden and set. Leave to cool for 15 minutes before removing from the tin. Dust with a little extra sugar to finish and cut into pieces while still a little warm. Delicious eaten fresh on the day or within 3 days.

Take a selection of shortbread to a casual coffee morning.

APPLE CINNAMON DIGESTIVES

A fruity twist on a classic English afternoon tea biscuit. To add a little twist, you can sandwich the biscuits with peanut butter or any other nut butter.

Makes 16 biscuits

75g spelt, kamut or whole wheat
    flour
75g porridge oats
1 teaspoon baking powder
75g brown sugar
1 teaspoon ground cinnamon
¼ teaspoon ground ginger
    (optional)
grating of nutmeg (optional)
pinch of sea salt
75g unsalted butter, plus extra for
    greasing
1 eating apple, coarsely grated

Preheat the oven to 180°C/356°F. Lightly grease a baking tray.

Combine the flour, oats, baking powder, sugar, spices and salt in a large bowl or food processor. Pulse the ingredients if using a food processor or rub together with your hands to mix well and lightly break up the oats.

Cut the butter into cubes and work into the mixture. Then add the apple, working it into the mixture until it comes together to form a dough. It shouldn't be too dry or too wet—add a little more flour if it's too wet or a little water.

Roll the dough into a log shape and chill in the freezer for 20 minutes. Cut into 1cm-thick rounds and shape each round into a circle about 5cm in diameter. Arrange on the prepared baking tray, leaving a 2cm gap between each biscuit and press as thin as possible—the thinner the biscuit, the crispier they will be. Bake for 10–12 minutes, or until golden and crisp around the edges.

Leave to cool for 1–2 minutes, then remove from the tray. When cool, store in an airtight container for up to 1 week.

TIP: *For biscuits on tap and last minute gifting, double up the recipe and make an extra log of dough to store in the freezer. You can then cut through the dough with a large, sharp knife and bake from frozen, cooking for 1-2 minutes longer to account for the chilliness of the dough.*

RHUBARB GINGER BISCUITS

Ginger biscuits are one of my staple recipes and I know lots of friends and family who'd vote them No. 1, too. I've been making all sorts of different versions over the years and have developed the various recipes to create something that's both delicious and a little healthier. To play with the classic rhubarb and ginger pairing, I've managed to weave in a little of the tangy fruit, which really works in my opinion, but you could easily swap it out for half an apple or 3 finely chopped dried apricots (or mango!), or leave the fruit out entirely.

Makes 16 biscuits

75g brown or coconut sugar
75g softened butter or coconut oil
2 tablespoons molasses or honey
125g spelt, kamut or whole wheat
   flour
¾ teaspoon baking powder
1 teaspoon ground cinnamon
1 teaspoon ground ginger
½ teaspoon ground cloves
pinch of sea salt
125g fresh rhubarb, finely diced

Preheat the oven to 180°C/356°F.

In a bowl, whisk the sugar, butter, molasses and egg yolk until smooth, light and a little creamy. In a separate bowl, mix all the dry ingredients together, then add them to the wet mix. Fold the rhubarb through the dough.

Roll the dough into a log shape and chill in the freezer for 20 minutes. Cut into 1cm-thick rounds and shape each round into a circle about 5cm in diameter. Arrange on the prepared baking tray, leaving a 2cm gap between each biscuit. Press as thin as possible.

Bake for 10–12 minutes until golden and crisp around the edges. Leave to cool on the tray, then wrap up and offer to your favorite ginger biscuit-loving friend.

PEANUT BUTTER & BANANA BISCUITS

A healthy take on classic peanut butter biscuits with a sweet fruity twist. Similarly to the Apple Cinnamon Digestives on page 102, the dough can be frozen and cooked straight from the freezer for a last minute treat. Simply increase the cooking time by 1–2 minutes.

Makes 12 biscuits

2 ripe bananas
200g pitted dates, chopped
2 tablespoons coconut oil
5 tablespoons peanut butter
  (smooth or crunchy, up to you) or
  cashew butter or almond butter
2 teaspoons vanilla extract
½ teaspoon ground cinnamon
pinch of sea salt
75g spelt or buckwheat flour
1 teaspoon baking powder
12 large chocolate buttons

Preheat the oven to 200°C/392°F.

Peel the bananas. Blend or purée (or chop and really mash them up) with the dates, coconut oil and peanut butter. Beat in the vanilla extract, cinnamon and salt.

Sift the flour and baking powder together and gently fold through the puréed fruit mixture.

Chill in the fridge for 30 minutes (this will make the mixture easier to shape). Line a baking tray with greaseproof paper.

Roll the mixture into 12 balls, then press each into a 1cm thick circle. Press a chocolate button into the center of each circle.

Bake on the top shelf for 10–15 minutes, or until set and a little golden around the edges. Leave to cool before eating. They will keep for 3 days in an airtight container.

Present these biscuits along with the recipe written out on a nice card so the recipient can recreate them for themselves!

MAYAN CHOCOLATE BISCUITS

These chocolate biscuits are almost like a cross between a chocolate truffle in their richness, yet balanced with a light-as-air meringue-like texture. Any chocolate lover will fall over themselves to receive these as a gift.

Makes 12–15 biscuits

2 tablespoons unsalted butter
100g dark chocolate, chopped
1 egg, separated
4 tablespoons coconut sugar,
   molasses or brown sugar
½ teaspoon ground cinnamon
pinch of chili powder or ground
   chipotle chili
pinch of sea salt

Preheat the oven to 180°C/356°F.

Put the butter and chocolate in a heatproof bowl over a saucepan of simmering water (do not let the bowl touch the water) until the chocolate has melted.

Whisk the egg white with a pinch of salt until light, fluffy and meringue-like.

Whisk the yolk, sugar and spices with an electric mixer or handheld electric whisk for about 5 minutes until the mixture lightens. Spoon the melted chocolate into the yolk mixture and whisk until smooth and glossy.

Fold the egg white through the mixture, little by little, until fully incorporated. The mixture will be quite thick.

Dollop 12–15 rounded teaspoons of the dough on a lightly greased baking tray, leaving space between each biscuit. Bake for 5–7 minutes, or until the biscuits are set and a little cracked on top.

Cool before removing from the tray. Finish with a pinch of sea salt if you like.

A vintage box, such as the cigar box pictured, gives these biscuits a really luxurious feel.

CASHEW BUTTER BLONDIES

My local café sells a version of these that I love, and every time my friends come round for coffee they bring me a little box to cheer me and keep me sweet, and that they certainly do!

Makes 12 blondies

170g cashew butter
1 egg
115g honey or maple syrup
50g coconut oil, plus extra for
    greasing
1 tablespoon freshly grated ginger
100g dark chocolate, chopped into
    small chunks

Preheat the oven to 180°C/356°F.

Mix the cashew butter, egg, honey, coconut oil and ginger in a large bowl until smooth.

Pour the batter into a greased 20cm square baking tin. Evenly scatter the chopped chocolate over the top, pressing it in a little as you do. Bake for 15–18 minutes. Allow to cool, then cut into 12 bars and serve.

RUSTIC JAM TARTS

I couldn't leave jam tarts out of this book. They are great to offer up at picnics or if I'm meeting a friend in the park in the summer. I love to fill the tarts with homemade jam too.

Makes 12 mini tarts

150g light rye or plain white flour
75g unsalted butter or coconut oil,
    cut into small cubes
pinch of sea salt
3–4 tablespoons cold water
250g jam of your choice or lemon
    curd

Preheat the oven to 180°C/356°F.

In a large bowl, rub together the flour, butter and salt until the texture resembles fine breadcrumbs. Add the water, little by little, to form a dough. Put in the freezer to firm up for 20 minutes.

Divide into 12 balls and press into the cups of a small muffin tin. Fill with jam or curd and bake for 20 minutes until golden. Remove from the oven and cool. Keep jam filled tarts for 2–3 days at room temperature, or store in the fridge if you've used curd.

TRIO OF SNACKING NUTS

Nuts are a brilliant gift at Christmas or to bring to a picnic or drinks party.

Each recipe makes 200g

PERSIAN LEMON PISTACHIOS

juice of 1 lemon
1 tablespoon olive oil
pinch of saffron threads
pinch of sea salt
200g pistachios
a pinch of chili flakes (optional)

HONEY NUT CLUSTERS

4 tablespoons honey
200g mixed nuts or your
    favorite nut
pinch of chili powder (optional)
pinch of finely chopped rosemary
    leaves (optional)
pinch of sea salt

KIMCHI-COATED NUTS

4 tablespoons kimchi brine
200g mixed nuts or your
    favorite nut

PERSIAN LEMON PISTACHIOS

Preheat the oven to 180°C/356°F. Whisk the lemon juice, oil, saffron and sea salt. Toss the pistachios in to coat. Arrange on a baking tray in a single layer. Roast for 20 minutes, or until the pistachios are lightly golden, crisp and fragrant.

HONEY NUT CLUSTERS

Preheat the oven to 180°C/356°F. Warm the honey in a small saucepan until just softened. Toss with the nuts to coat fully. Add the chili powder and rosemary (if using) and the salt. Arrange in clusters on a baking tray. Roast for 20 minutes, or until the nuts are lightly golden, crisp and fragrant.

KIMCHI-COATED NUTS

Preheat the oven to 180°C/356°F. Toss the kimchi brine and nuts together. Arrange on a baking tray in a single layer. Roast for 20 minutes, or until the nuts are lightly golden, crisp and fragrant.

VERYAN'S MOLASSES GRANOLA

This wonderful recipe is from my dear friend Veryan Wilkie-Jones, who has gifted me numerous batches of this gorgeous granola over the years. Her use of molasses in this recipe gives the granola a simple, understated sweetness and a wonderful, almost smoky flavor.

Makes 1.2kg

800g oats
250g seeds of your choice (I use
   a mixture of pumpkin, sunflower
   and linseed)
85ml olive oil
50ml rapeseed oil
75ml molasses
75ml date syrup or clear honey

Preheat the oven to 150°C/302°F.

Put the oats and seeds in a large roasting tin, then pour over the remaining ingredients.

Bake for 15–20 minutes until the mixture has warmed up and become easy to stir. Give the mixture a really thorough stir with a large wooden spoon or spatula until all the oats are coated.

Return to the oven and give the mixture a good stir every 30 minutes to ensure the granola cooks evenly. The cooking time is 1½–2 hours.

Give the mixture one last stir, then turn off the oven and return the tin to the oven with the door closed to crisp up until cool.

Store in an airtight container to maintain some crunch. If need be, you can always cook it again in the oven (same temperature) for around 10 minutes and let it crisp up again.

Package in simple kraft brown paper bags with see-through windows and secure with tin ties.

TEMPER

Chocolate is very sensitive to temperature and if it gets too warm, it can become grainy or lose its gloss. Tempering chocolate can stop this happening, and it is easy to do at home if you follow these simple steps.

Find a saucepan that you can fit a glass or metal bowl over. Fill the pan a quarter full of simmering water and set over a low heat.

Make sure the bowl is clean and dry. Set it over the simmering water, making sure the base doesn't touch the water. Roughly chop the chocolate and place two-thirds of it in the bowl. Let it melt slowly without stirring.

Remove the pan from the heat once two-thirds of the chocolate in the bowl has melted. Stir until all the chocolate in the bowl has melted.

Add the remaining one-third of chocolate. Remove the bowl from the pan and rest it on a tea towel—this will help cool the bowl down.

Stir gently until all the chocolate has melted. The chocolate will begin to thicken and become less shiny as it cools. Be patient as this can take up to 30 minutes, but it'll be worth the wait.

Once fully melted, use straight away. If it starts to set, you can set the bowl over the simmering water again, but just let it melt again really slowly over the lowest heat possible. Perfectly tempered chocolate should never reach above 31°C/88°F for dark chocolate, 30°C/86°F for milk chocolate and 27°C/81°F for white chocolate.

JASMINE TRUFFLES

I used to work for a tea company called Jing. They source the most exquisite jasmine pearl tea. The tea is made by hand-rolling tea leaves into little pearls when they are fresh and young in the spring. They are dried and stored until summer when a fragrant flush of jasmine flowers is then harvested and used to perfume the tea leaves. This is repeated over a few days to imbue the leaves with the heavenly scent of jasmine. When brewed as a tea and married with white chocolate, the combination makes the most decadent truffle.

Makes 16 truffles

200g white chocolate
2 tablespoons good-quality
   jasmine green tea leaves
100ml boiling water
50ml cold water
100g icing sugar, for dusting
2 tablespoons jasmine tea leaves,
   to garnish (optional)

Break the chocolate into small pieces. Add two-thirds of the chocolate to a heatproof bowl set over a saucepan filled one-quarter full of boiling water. Make sure the bowl doesn't touch the water. Melt very slowly until just melted, don't be tempted to stir. Once melted, add the remaining chocolate and remove from the heat and stir until the remaining chocolate has melted.

Pour the boiling water and cold water over the tea leaves and steep for 15 minutes. Strain the tea (discarding the leaves), measure 40ml of tea and then vigorously whisk it into the melted chocolate until you have a silky mixture. Pop in the freezer for 20 minutes, or until firm.

Meanwhile (if using) grind the jasmine tea leaves in a coffee grinder or pestle and mortar. Add to the icing sugar and grind together to make a fragrant sugar.

Once the truffle mixture has set, scoop it into 16 teaspoon-sized balls and roll through the sugar to coat thoroughly. Pop in the fridge or freezer to set further. Best stored in the fridge until ready to eat. Will keep for up to 1 week.

MARMALADE & TOAST TRUFFLES

Marmalade on toast with salted butter is one of my ultimate comforts and I know I'm not alone, therefore, making these gorgeous truffles is perfect for any marmalade-lover in your life. Everyone I've gifted these to has fallen madly in love with them.

Makes about 12 truffles

100ml single cream or almond milk
50g marmalade
200g dark chocolate, finely
  chopped
¼ teaspoon ground cinnamon
pinch of sea salt
100g breadcrumbs or 50g slice of
  toast
1 tablespoon unsalted butter

In a small saucepan, warm the cream with the marmalade. Put the chocolate in a bowl, and stir the warm cream through the chocolate. Set the bowl over a saucepan with a little simmering water, if needed, to help melt the chocolate. Let it melt slowly.

If your chocolate splits, spoon the mix into a food processor with 2 tablespoons boiling water and blend until smooth, or whip the water in by hand with a whisk until the mix comes together again.

Chill the chocolate mixture until firm. Roll into 12 balls. Mix the ground cinnamon and salt into the toast crumbs. Melt the butter in a large frying pan. Add the toast crumbs and gently fry until just golden. Allow to cool, then roll the truffles through the toast crumbs.

Chill until ready to serve. Will keep for 1 week in the fridge, though best eaten at room temperature.

BESPOKE BARS & BUTTONS

Making homemade chocolate bars and buttons peppered with a loved one's favorite spices, herbs, nuts, seeds, dried fruit or other flavors is so much fun and always gratefully received. They're also so simple to make.

Makes 2 x 100g bars or 12 large buttons

200g dark, milk or white chocolate flavors of your choice (see below for ideas)
chocolate molds or greaseproof paper

FLAVOR IDEAS

Spanish: a rich milk chocolate with orange zest and ground cinnamon and toasted marcona almonds

Tropical: dark chocolate with dried mango, pineapple, toasted cashews and coconut flakes

Persian: white chocolate with powdered saffron and ground cardamom, topped with crushed pistachios

Italian: dark chocolate mixed with fresh or dried lemon zest, topped with cacao nibs and crushed hazelnuts

American: milk chocolate topped with crushed salted peanuts and pretzels

Have your flavorings to hand and your chocolate molds ready, or a baking tray or chopping board lined with greaseproof paper at the ready.

Organize your flavorings.

Temper the chocolate according to the instructions on page 112.

Pour the chocolate into the molds, filling just below the rim. If you're making buttons, dollop 2 teaspoons of the melted chocolate on the greaseproof paper and let it spread into a large circle, or help spread it using the back of a spoon—not too thin—leaving 2–3cm of space around each button.

Scatter your flavorings evenly over the top. Pop in the fridge or freezer to set for 30 minutes to 1 hour. Remove from the mold or greaseproof paper and pop into a greaseproof or tissue paper-lined box or into a pretty container or wrap individually.

They will keep for 1 week to 10 days stored at room temperature.

PERSIAN PISTACHIO BUTTER CUPS

My ultimate childhood treat was frozen Reese's Peanut Butter Cups. I find the commercial version a little too sweet these days and typically make my own peanut butter cups. I have since ventured into making nut butter cups with all sorts of different nut butters. A friend of mine has a smokehouse and makes the most incredible smoked cashew butter. If you can get hold of something similar or if you've simply got peanut, almond, cashew or any nut or seed butter (even tahini), you can swap it out for the pistachio butter (and change up the spices, or omit them entirely, too). This pistachio version is a winner and when I make these cups for friends they always beg for more (and for the recipe).

Makes 8–10 cups

200g dark or milk chocolate
6 tablespoons pistachio butter
2 tablespoons coconut oil
2 teaspoons rose water
ground seeds from 6 cardamom
   pods
2 teaspoons honey or maple syrup
12 mini or 6 larger cupcake cases
   (silicone cases work best)
rose petals or crushed pistachios,
   to garnish (optional)

Chop the chocolate into small pieces. Place in a glass or metal bowl. Rest the bowl on a saucepan that is ¼ full of boiling water. On a low heat, stir the chocolate until half melted. Take off the heat. Stir until fully melted.

Spoon half the chocolate into mini silicone cupcake or chocolate cases. Tilt them and use the back of a spoon to coat the sides of the cases, creating an outer shell of chocolate. Pop them in the fridge or freezer until set.

Whip the pistachio butter with the coconut oil, rose water, cardamom and honey. Spoon the mixture into each case, almost to the top and smooth it down.

Top each case with melted chocolate, covering the pistachio butter mixture. Garnish with rose petals or crushed pistachios if you have any. Chill to set.

Delicious cold or at room temperature. These cups keep for up to 1 week, or you can freeze them for up to 3 months in an airtight container.

HONEY BUNNIES

One Christmas I gave my son a child's chocolate making lesson at Paul A. Young's first shop in north London. Paul is an amazing chocolatier and what I loved about his course is that it didn't dumb down the instruction for kids. Even better, parents were invited to stay for the session, where we covered tempering and making chocolates in molds. After the course, I bought my son some silicone chocolate molds, one of which was bunny-shaped. For Easter, we make these honey-filled chocolate bunnies to give out as gifts, and to eat ourselves. If you can find some colored foil you can wrap them up and use them in place of eggs for Easter hunts.

  If you don't have bunny-shaped chocolate molds you can use any shape … eggs are nice, but you can even reuse the trays shop-bought chocolates come in.

Makes 12 bunnies

300g dark or a good-quality milk
 chocolate
150g clear honey
pinch of sea salt

Temper half the chocolate (see page 112). Drizzle the chocolate into the bunny molds, adding just enough to coat the bottom and sides. Pop in the fridge to set.

Once set, fill each bunny two-thirds with honey, ensuring you leave enough space to pour the final layer of chocolate later. Pop the honey-filled bunnies in the fridge for 30 minutes.

Temper the remaining chocolate so that it is ready when your honey-filled bunnies come out of the fridge. Carefully spoon the chocolate over the top of each bunny. Pop back in the fridge to set.

When the chocolate is set, carefully remove from the molds and wrap, bundle into little bags or arrange in a paper-lined box. These will keep for 1 week, but if the chocolate isn't tempered it will lose its sheen and snap.

Divide the bunnies into 3 or 4 small paper bags for the perfect treat for little ones.

DRY

Drying fruit, vegetables, herbs and more is so easy and the results are hugely versatile.

You don't need an expensive dehydrator to dry fresh produce. You can simply use the warmth from the sun, a radiator or the heat of an oven set on a low temperature.

Pat the fruit or veg dry, thinly slice, arrange on a clean tea towel and set in a warm, dry place for a week, or until fully dried.

Or, for faster results, and in areas prone to predators (i.e. cats or if you're worried about attracting fruit flies), you can arrange the thin slices of fruit or veg on a greaseproof paper-lined baking tray and dry in a 100°C/212°F oven for an hour, or until fully dried, turning once or twice to dry evenly and prevent sticking.

The best way to store is in a clean and super-dry jar—one that is not warm (as this can cause condensation and mold). Cap the jar with a clean piece of cloth and a ribbon or rubber band (at least for the first month or so after making). This means that if there is any residual moisture it can escape. I once dried a huge batch of nettles, packed them into a jar and secured it, airtight with a lid, only to find the contents mildewed as they hadn't fully dried.

HORSERADISH SALT

This is like mustard powder, but better in my mind, especially if you've grown or foraged the root yourself. The first time I made this was after a friend dug up an enormous root on a blustery day on the edge of autumn. I infused some of the root in vodka (see page 27) and then I grated, dried and powdered the rest. It's the perfect gift for anyone who likes experimenting with flavors, for those who love spice and people fond of a good Bloody Mary.

Makes approx. 70g

1 horseradish root
few pinches of sea salt, to taste

Wash, dry, peel and finely grate the horseradish root (or you can chop it into fairly small pieces—the latter will take longer to dry). Arrange in a single layer on a wooden chopping board or on a cloth-lined baking tray.

Dry at room temperature for 1 week, or in the oven at 75°C/167°F for 1–2 hours, or until fully dried but not colored. Leave the horseradish to cool completely if you used the oven to dry it. Grind it to a powder in a coffee grinder and add a little salt to taste.

Give a batch of this to someone along with a list of possible uses: whipped into aioli and spread over roasted parsnips; stirred into hollandaise alongside steak or smoked haddock; sprinkled over mushroom and thyme soup; dusted over a beetroot risotto; or rubbed into a joint of beef or lamb before roasting.

VEGETABLE STOCK POWDER

This is a lovely gift and one I love receiving. My Italian friend Grazia introduced me to it as she always brings a jar back after visiting home. It's so much better than shop-bought stock cubes and having it to hand means you can whip up homemade soup with a beautiful stock in minutes.

Makes 100g

2 large carrots
4 celery stalks
1 large onion
2 garlic cloves
sea salt (5 percent of the weight of
    your vegetables)
1 teaspoon fennel seeds
1 teaspoon coriander seeds
5 black peppercorns
5 dried bay leaves

Preheat the oven to 100°C/212°F. Wash, dry and coarsely grate your vegetables or blitz in a food-processor until finely chopped.

Weigh the vegetables and add 5 percent of the weight in salt. The veg should weigh around 600g, meaning you'd need 30g salt.

Spread the mixture in a thin layer (about 1cm deep or less, if possible) on a large baking tray—or divide between two trays if needed. Place in the oven on the top shelf, or one on the top and one in the middle, if using two. Bake in the preheated oven for 2 hours or until dry and slightly crispy. Stir every half an hour and if you used two trays, swap them around half way during cooking.

Once the vegetables are cool, put them in a coffee grinder, ideally, or a food-processor with the spices and bay leaves (grind these in a pestle and mortar first if you're using a food processor) and blitz to a powder.

Store the vegetable stock powder in a glass jar. For the first week cover with a thick piece of cloth, just in case there's any residual moisture, then secure with an airtight lid for 3 months. To make stock, use 1 tablespoon powder per 500ml boiling water.

OVEN-DRIED TOMATOES

Sun-dried or oven-dried tomatoes are a great source of the antioxidant lycopene, vitamins C and K, and iron. Their flavor and nutrients are very concentrated, so they pack a lot of nutritional value into a small package!

Makes 100g

250g cherry tomatoes
pinch of sea salt

Preheat the oven to 100°C/212°F. Halve the tomatoes and arrange on a grill tray or baking sheet, cut-side up. Dust with the salt. Cook for 3–4 hours, or until shrivelled and dried. Finish drying at room temperature for 1–2 days (lightly cover with cheesecloth, if needed, to protect them from any preying insects).

Once fully dried, store in a jar covered with a cloth (this prevents the tomatoes from going moldy should there still be any residual moisture). Keep at room temperature for up to 1 year.

HOME-DRIED MUSHROOMS

I think dried mushrooms are almost better than fresh ones as you get such a concentration of flavor. They're brilliant in risottos, stews and soups, or grind to a powder in a coffee grinder or a pestle and mortar and use to dust over scrambled eggs, knead into bread, or sprinkle over pastry along with some cheese for posh mushroom cheese straws.

Makes 100g

400g mushrooms
pinch of chopped herbs (rosemary, thyme or fennel fronds)

Thinly slice the mushrooms. Line a chopping board or baking tray with a clean tea towel. Arrange the mushroom slices in a single layer—avoid any overlapping. For added flavor, dust with finely chopped herbs.

Leave in a warm, dry place for 4–5 days, or until fully dried. Next to a radiator is a good spot, or dry in a 100°C/212°F oven for 1–2 hours, or until fully dried, turning once or twice to ensure even drying and to prevent sticking.

Once dry, place in sterilized jars (see page 78) and cover with a clean piece of cloth. After they have been left for a further 2 weeks, place an airtight lid on the jar and keep for up to 1 year.

NOURISHING POT NOODLES

These make amazing "Get Well Soon" gifts for friends who are under the weather. They're also brilliant for new parents who need easy nourishment after the arrival of a little one, or for friends who've just moved and don't have a fully functioning kitchen yet. I love having a stash of them before and after Christmas, too, as I'm usually out and about and in need of something quick to eat once I've come in from the cold.

Makes 1 x 500g jar

1 stock cube or 1 tablespoon
  Vegetable Stock Powder (see
  page 126)
75g vermicelli or pad Thai rice
  noodles
choice of flavoring (see below)

THE FLAVORS

Italian pot noodle:

2 tablespoons oven- or sun-dried
  tomatoes (see page 127)
1–2 tablespoons dried mushrooms
  (see page 128)
½ teaspoon dried basil, rosemary
  or thyme
1 tablespoon dried nettle leaves
  (optional)

Curried kale:

2 tablespoons dried kale
2 tablespoons dried grated carrot
  and/or parsnip
1 teaspoon curry powder
pinch of chili flakes (optional)

Simply bundle the ingredients in a dry, clean jar—clip-top Kilner jars are ideal. When ready to make, top up with enough boiling water to cover. Stir and set aside to steep for 5 minutes before eating.

Make sure the jars aren't cold when you add the boiling water. In the winter the room temperature can make them too cold and prone to cracking once you add the boiling water. If you're worried about this, tip the contents into a bowl before adding the water.

Write up instructions for how to turn these nourishing little pots from a collection of dry ingredients to a delicious meal for the recipient to follow and attach to each jar.

SPICE BLENDS

THE BEST CURRY POWDER

This is inspired by the wonderful Gunpowder restaurant in London, a gorgeous Indian restaurant inspired by family recipes. Use it as a base for curries, to dust over meat and veg for grilling, add to salad dressings or to swirl through homemade mayonnaise for a spicy dip.

Makes 70g

2 tablespoons coriander seeds; 2 tablespoons cumin seeds; 1 teaspoon black peppercorns; 15 cardamom pods; 5 dried bay leaves; 1 cinnamon stick; 1 whole nutmeg; 1 teaspoon fennel seeds; 1 teaspoon cloves; 1 teaspoon caraway seeds; 2 tablespoons ground turmeric; 1 teaspoon ground ginger; ½ teaspoon sea salt

Set a frying pan over a medium heat and add all the ingredients, apart from the ground turmeric and ginger. Toast for about 2 minutes until fragrant and lightly toasted. Remove from the pan and allow the spices cool. Grind to a powder, then fold in the ground turmeric, ginger and salt. Spoon into a jar and allow to fully cool before securing an airtight lid. It will keep for up to 1 year.

ZA'ATAR

I could put this gorgeous Middle Eastern spice and seed mix on just about anything. What I love about it is that you can make your own using herbs you've grown or foraged, like thyme or oregano and sumac.

Makes 70g

4 tablespoons toasted sesame seeds; 4 tablespoons dried thyme and/or oregano; 4 tablespoons sumac; 2 tablespoons ground cumin; ½ teaspoon sea salt

Mix everything together and store in an airtight jar. Rub into whole roast chicken, dust over hummus, toss with roasted carrots or sprinkle over roasted kale crisps.

HOME-GROWN ROSE HARISSA

This is a stunning spice blend made with dried chilies, dried lemon balm or lemon verbena, and dried rose petals. Add a few spices and you've got a pretty special spice blend which is great for adding to soups, dips, pickles, chutneys and more. After being invited to harvest chilies from my friend's allotment, I dried my harvest and made this as gift to thank him for sharing his harvest.

Makes 70g

30g dried chilies
5g dried lemon balm, lemon
  verbena or mint leaves
3 tablespoons dried rose petals
1 tablespoon fennel seeds, toasted
1 tablespoon coriander seeds,
  toasted
1 tablespoon cumin seeds, toasted
1 tablespoon ground cinnamon
½ freshly grated nutmeg
½ teaspoon sea salt

Grind all the ingredients in a coffee or spice grinder until you have a fine powder.

Cool fully (as the grinding will have heated the mix up a bit) before spooning into an airtight jar.

Store in a cool, dark place for up to 1 year.

HERB POWDERS

My mother is an amazing herb gardener, an incredible cook and a keen preserver. Instead of just drying her rosemary, she whizzes it into a powder (after it's dried), which offers so much more flavor. She always gives me a jar and every time I use it, I think of sitting on her porch at sunrise watching the birds. These are my three favorite herb powders, but you can apply this method to any herbs, leaf or flower—just dry fully and grind, then mix with salt or sugar, or use on its own.

ROSEMARY POWDER
5g dried rosemary yields 1 tablespoon powder.

Uses: delicious dusted over roasted root vegetables, sprinkled on fish, mixed through butter to top a steak or to spread on toast, added to bread dough or to dumplings for chicken soup.

NETTLE POWDER
5g dried nettles yields 1 tablespoon powder.

Uses: smoothies, soups, pasta dough or pasta fillings (mix with goat's cheese or ricotta).

BAY LEAF POWDER
5g dried bay leaves yields 1 tablespoon powder.

I have a vase of bay branches with dried leaves. When my stash of bay leaf powder gets low, I just grab a bundle of leaves from a branch and blitz them to a powder in my coffee grinder.

Uses: dauphinoise potatoes; rubbed on roast chicken, beef, lamb, pork, venison, game birds; dusted over dips, soups; rolled into pasta; cakes (especially with apple and rose), crumbles, homemade ice cream, panna cotta; mixed with sugar and dusted over shortbread.

GARDEN TEAS & HERBS

In the summer, my garden produces an abundance of oregano, rosemary, lemon verbena, various varieties of mint and lemon balm, and heaps of lavender. I have bundles of lavender I gathered in the summer hanging ribbon-tied in my sitting room, and in my kitchen are jars of dried lemon verbena, mints, lemon balm, foraged linden blossom, dog rose petals and calendula petals. These make wonderful teas, and packed in a pretty jar with a ribbon and tag noting brewing instructions, they make great gifts. See what combinations you can create.

PERSIAN DRIED LIMES

You can hardly call this a recipe but it's certainly worth noting the joys of dried limes. To create this wonderful ingredient—used to perfume rice and stews in Iran—you simply leave whole limes to dry at room temperature (around 18-20°C/64-68°F) until the skin is fully hardened and the center sounds hollow. I normally leave mine for 9 months to 1 year, which seems a very long time, but time seems to fly so quickly, and it's a very hands-off project. They're well worth making. Not only are they gorgeous in lamb stews or with rice, traditional Persian style, you can also infuse them in gin or oil, or you can powder them to make spectacular Persian dried sugar or salt to tart up sweet or savory dishes, like adding to cakes or pairing with hummus. You can also dry small lemons this way—Beldi lemons from Morocco, which are traditionally used to make preserved lemons, work a treat.

ROSY TURMERIC SPICE MIX

My dear friend Rebecca Sullivan featured a recipe for turmeric chai with rose in her book *The Art of Edible Herbs*, which is a really stunning book full of inspiring ideas. I often whip up spice blends to give to friends, and it's a great gift for new mothers, birthdays and as a get-well remedy. Beyond tea, the mix can be swirled into porridge, added to shortbread, flapjacks, cakes and other bakes, whisked into a dressing, used in fermented drinks like water kefir or kombucha, in soups and much more. Make individual servings or upscale to as many servings as you like and fill a jam jar.

Makes 70g

40g ground turmeric
16 whole cardamom pods
10 black peppercorns
5g ground ginger
10g dried rose petals or rose buds
15g ground cinnamon or cinnamon
   sticks

Grind everything in a coffee grinder or a pestle and mortar to a fine powder. If you're using a coffee grinder, add the cardamom pods whole, or just use the seeds if you're grinding by hand.

Gift with instructions for use: "Warm 250 milk with 1 heaped teaspoon spice mix in a saucepan until warmed through and a little steamy. Add 1 teaspoon coconut oil (optional) and sweeten to taste with 1 teaspoon honey or maple syrup. Add more spice mix for a stronger flavor."

CARDAMOM & LIME BANANA CHIPS

My son doesn't like bananas, but when I first made these he ate the entire batch. I wouldn't recommend that, however, there's something to be said for the child-friendliness of these little treats. They're the perfect gift for kids, students or new mothers looking for nourishing treats.

Makes about 40 slices

zest and juice of 1 lime
Crushed seeds from 4 cardamom
  pods
3 large bananas, sliced into
  5mm rounds
a little olive oil or coconut oil, if
  using a baking sheet

Preheat the oven to 100°C/212°F. Combine the lime zest and juice, cardamom and bananas in a large bowl. Arrange in an even layer on a lightly oiled baking tray. Bake on the top shelf for 2–3 hours, or until almost fully dried. They'll be a little chewy, so leave to dry at room temperature for up to 24 hours. Use the banana skins to make Banana Skin Vinegar (see page 44).

Store in a container with a little breathing space (a cardboard box or a jar with a fabric lid) to help the banana dry out further.

CINNAMON APPLE RINGS

These make the perfect snack, especially for little ones. They can also be added to porridge, or taken for a treat on-the-go.

Makes about 40 slices

pinch of sea salt
6 apples
dusting of ground cinnamon

Mix 500ml water with the sea salt in a large bowl. Core and thinly slice the apples, dropping into the water as you go.

Arrange the slices on a wire rack. Dry at room temperature for 4–5 days or in a 100°C/212°F oven for 1–2 hours until fully dried. Turn once or twice to dry evenly and prevent sticking. Store in a sterilized jar (see page 78) securely covered with cloth.

ROASTED PLUM LEATHERS

I've always loved the idea of fruit leather, but was put off making it as most recipes require either a dehydrator or hours of cooking at a low heat in a conventional oven. These plum leathers are brilliant as they only take an hour to set and the recipe is hugely flexible. Swap the plums out for apples, quince or summer stone fruit (such as peaches and apricots). For a boozy adult version use sloe gin rather than honey to sweeten the mixture. Or add strained sloes from sloe gin to the plums towards the end of roasting to ensure nothing goes to waste.

Makes 12–15 fruit leather roll-ups

400g plums, quartered and stoned
a few sprigs of fresh herbs, flowers
  or spices (optional)
1–2 tablespoons honey or maple
  syrup (more or less, to taste)

FLAVOR OPTIONS

lavender and lemon verbena
star anise and ginger
ginger, cardamom and cinnamon
sloe gin

Preheat the oven to 200°C/392°F. Arrange the plums in a roasting tin with herbs, flowers or spices of your choice (see left).

Roast for 20 minutes, or until the plums have fully cooked down and look like a compote. Add enough honey to sweeten it to your taste. Roast for a further 5–10 minutes.

Remove any whole herbs or spices. Scrape the mixture into a bowl or saucepan and blend with a stick blender, or transfer to a blender or food processor and blend until smooth. Press the mixture through a fine-mesh sieve to remove the plum skins, giving you a smooth purée.

Reduce the oven to 100°C/212°F. Line a large baking tray with greaseproof paper. Spoon a scant tablespoon of the mixture onto the paper. Smooth with the back of the spoon to make a thin biscuit-like circle—as thin as 2mm or less, and 7cm in diameter. Repeat with the remaining mixture, leaving a little room between each leather.

Cook on the top shelf of the oven for 1 hour, or until the fruit leathers look fully dry. Leave to cool for at least 15 minutes before removing from the paper. Alternatively, just cut the paper around the leathers, roll up and store in a jam jar or tie with string and save for later. They're a brilliant snack for adults and kids.

TIP: *Scrape all the sieved pulp, stones and herbs, flower or spice scraps into a clean jar and cover with apple cider vinegar or white wine vinegar. Leave to infuse for 1 month to 1 year. Strain, bottle, label and give! See the Infuse chapter (pages 12-31) for more ideas on infused vinegars.*

INDEX

ACKNOWLEDGMENTS

There are always so many people that feed into the process of crafting a tome and it's always really tricky to pull the first name out of that hat, but I think Federica Leonardis deserves the first mention for so many reasons. Not only the best literary agent a writer could wish for, she's also a wonderful friend and a brilliant sounding board for all my ideas.

This book of course wouldn't exist without the lovely team, a family of sorts, at Kyle Books. This is my third book with you and I really hope we do lots more together. To Judith Hannam and Joanna Copestick for commissioning such beautiful books, to Kyle Cathie, who started it all and to my talented editor Hannah Coughlin, who is as thoughtful as she is thorough, and has the patience of a saint. A huge amount of love goes out to photographer Ali Allen (plus her wonderful and unbelievably adorable kitten, Lily), who is such a lovely person to spend time with whilst making it all come to life. And to Rachel Cross, for her gorgeous design. A special mention to Kelly Shearer for helping me style the shoots and for brining so many gorgeous props, including your gorgeous handmade ceramics, and Julia Thompson who helped shaped the manuscript.

My beautiful son Rory is always worthy of pages of praise. He's not only tried every recipe and witnessed the failed attempts at things that didn't make the cut, but he's an incredible and inspiring cook in his own right and he is by far the best gift I've ever received.

I also want to thank my beautiful family and my amazing friends who've helped inspire me and the recipes in this book. Special mentions go to Sara Haglund, Laura Marchant-Short and Rebecca Sullivan for all the beautiful gifts you've given me over the years, most importantly that being the gift of friendship. Also, enormous thanks to Veryan Wilkie-Jones and Sanchia Lovell for their gorgeous recipes. And, of course, my mother Jeannine, sisters Robin and Skipper, brother Marshall, all their broods, and my wonderful grandparents Ima and Lloyd, for being the most inspiring cooks and gardeners I know. My family always create magic in the kitchen and beyond; they are the foundation from which I've built a lovely career in food. Thank you, I love you all more than you could possibly know.

First published in Great Britain in 2019 by
Kyle Books, an imprint of Kyle Cathie Ltd
Carmelite House, 50 Victoria Embankment
London EC4Y 0DZ
www.kylebooks.co.uk

ISBN: 9781440355011

Published in North America by Betterway Books, an imprint of
Penguin Random House LLC
www.penguinrandomhouse.com

Publisher: Joanna Copestick
Editor: Hannah Coughlin
Design: Rachel Cross
Photography and prop styling: Ali Allen
Food styling: Rachel de Thample
Production: Emily Noto

Printed and bound in China

10 9 8 7 6 5 4 3 2 1